A 30-Day Journey

WEAVING
A LIFE
of
PRAYER

Marsha Crockett

InterVarsity Press
Downers Grove, Illinois

InterVarsity Press
P.O. Box 1400, Downers Grove, IL 60515
World Wide Web: www.ivpress.com
E-mail: mail@ivpress.com

InterVarsity Press® is the book-publishing division of InterVarsity Christian Fellowship/USA®, a student movement active on campus at hundreds of universities, colleges and schools of nursing in the United States of America, and a member movement of the International Fellowship of Evangelical Students. For information about local and regional activities, write Public Relations Dept., InterVarsity Christian Fellowship/USA, 6400 Schroeder Rd., P.O. Box 7895, Madison, WI 53707-7895.

Cover illustration: Judith T. Yamamoto

ISBN 0-8308-1949-5

Printed in the United States of America

Library of Congress Cataloging-in-Publication Data

Crockett, Marsha, 1957-
    Weaving a life of prayer : a 30-day journey / Marsha Crockett.
      p. cm.
    ISBN 0-8308-1949-5 (pbk. : alk. paper)
    1. Christian women—Prayer-books and devotions—English.   2. Women
in the Bible—Meditations.   3. Devotional calendars.   I. Title.
BV4844.C696   1998
242'.843—dc21
                                              98-16741
                                                CIP

21 20 19 18 17 16 15 14 13 12 11 10 9 8 7 6 5 4 3 2 1

16 15 14 13 12 11 10 09 08 07 06 05 04 03 02 01 00 99 98

Acknowledgments

I'm always amazed at how God sets people on the earth to cross our paths at our moments of greatest need. I want to acknowledge those people who have come alongside me in this journey and woven their lives into mine, making me stronger in so many ways.

First, the men and women whom I've never met but have touched my heart and taught me to see beyond the veil of prayer. There are too many to list here, but I am especially grateful to Emilie Griffin and Richard Foster. Thanks also to Jennifer Kennedy Dean, whose encouragement and insights into the life of prayer have inspired me.

My Tuesday morning writers group, Betty Arthurs, Linda Carlblom, Nancy Demmit, Andrea Huelsenbeck and Judy Robertson. Week after week you supported my efforts, sharpened my skills, raised the standard of excellence and prayed for me.

The men, women and children of Canyon Creek Community Church, who have become my family in Christ. They impart the grace of Jesus as they continue to allow me to grow and stretch my wings. Thanks especially to my pastor, Timm Jackson, and his wife, Karen, for their consistent love and encouragement.

My editor, Cindy Bunch-Hotaling, who held my hand through the hard parts of this process. I'm so grateful for your teaching spirit and encouraging heart.

My daughters, Megan and Amy. Thanks for being as proud of me as I am of you. You constantly amaze me with your insight and love.

John, my husband. You are my fearless champion in life. God knew what he was doing when he gave us to each other. You enrich me in so many ways, and I am eternally grateful.

Introduction: The Golden Thread

"Not again! What kind of Christian am I, God?" Lying in bed one night, I reflected on the ordinary events of the day. Frustration and guilt engulfed me, like the darkness surrounding me, when I realized I had failed, again, to pray even once during my hectic day. To be honest, God never even crossed my mind. I tossed and turned as I considered the difference it might have made if I had merely whispered his name. But my schedule and the demands of work veiled his presence to me for days, even weeks at a time. "I don't want to stumble around in this darkness any longer," I continued to pray.

I laughed at the thought of "praying without ceasing." Ceasing to pray wasn't my problem. Getting started was the bigger problem. I knew there had to be more to prayer than attending prayer meetings, saying grace at dinner and reciting the bedtime prayers of childhood. I longed to find another way, a more natural way, like everyday life. I wanted my prayer life to become a life of prayer, to breathe with the reality of God in the earthiness of my daily living.

In my quest to "figure it out," I began reading volumes of books on the subject of prayer. Each had its own idea about how, when and what would happen when I followed certain steps. But I felt as stilted as someone learning to dance by reading about ballet. Despite my awkwardness, one simple idea written by Ignatius of Loyola pro-foundly affected how I prayed: "Everything one turns in the direction of God is prayer."

This truth opened my eyes to a whole new world, where God lives in the ordinary events of life—where a frustrated young mother in the grocery checkout line prompts a prayer for Christ's peace surrounding me, where watching my husband interact with our daughters reveals the Father-heart of God toward me, and where an undeserved act of forgiveness releases God's grace within me.

Slowly, I began to turn toward God with other areas of my life—with yesterday's heartaches and today's challenges. I turned everything in his direction including my parenting skills, my marriage, my joys and my disappointments. I searched for God's face in the crowdedness of my life, and when I saw him there, he smiled and waved as if he'd been waiting to make eye contact, waiting for me to turn toward him so he could run to me.

Is there really a difference between a prayer life and a life of prayer? It's like the difference between buying frozen vegetables and nurturing a garden from seedlings to harvest, or the difference between watching a sitcom about married life and having a vital, intimate relationship with my spouse. The first way is easy, quick and noninteractive. The second is an ongoing, dynamic, life-breathing, give-and-take process, like the relationship God longs to nurture with me.

Perhaps the best analogy for a life of prayer lies in the threads of a tapestry, intricately woven into beautiful scenes and designs. Each thread pulls across the loom so tightly it's nearly impossible to see where one thread starts or stops. All seem woven as one to make a complete picture. If I could grasp that golden thread called prayer and somehow let God weave it into my life, then I'd begin to see how I too am woven as one with Christ. Not that I would forego regular quiet times set aside for prayer and devotion, but that somehow God would change my perception of this discipline, teaching me to bring it with me into real life.

In my desire to grow in this way, the lives of women in Scripture drew me into God's picture of prayer. Their lives became another thread of this prayer tapestry, adding color and texture and always turning me in his direction. This first thread in my tapestry, a mere longing, began a new way of praying, a way of making my life a prayer.

How to Use This Book

One of my favorite psalms calls us blessed "who have set [our] hearts on pilgrimage." (Psalm 84:5). A life of prayer is about a heart on pilgrimage—a heart always listening and watching for God's presence. Listen for his voice through Scripture, with a quiet heart. Listen to him in everyday events and routines and in a specific devotional time. Hear and see him in nature or at work in your church home. Let him speak through the people and circumstances he puts in your life.

The words I've written in this book are intended to stimulate your thoughts and broaden your attitude toward prayer beyond a "correct" way of praying. I share my own experiences to encourage you to open your life to God as an act of unceasing prayer every moment of the day and even as you sleep. So I offer these suggestions as you "weave" your way through these pages.

Commit to thirty days. Studies have concluded that it takes approximately twenty-one days of consistent activity to develop a habit. Here's your opportunity to solidify a lifestyle of unceasing prayer. Every fourth day the topic changes to give you another aspect of turning your life into a prayer. The challenges you read about during this thirty-day journey will not necessarily match your own life circumstances. While you may be reading about disappointment one day, your experience may be centered in success and victory. Let God speak to you wherever you are.

I encourage you to begin by working straight through the book to maintain the connection between chapters. In some places I refer back to topics already discussed in previous chapters. However, feel free to go to a specific topic later to help you in praying through a particular circumstance.

Read the text. At the beginning of each chapter is the Scripture text and story of a woman in the Bible—five from the Old Testament, five from the New Testament. Don't skip over these passages. Take time to slowly read through their lives and let them speak to you as they have spoken to me. Much of what I write in the chapters assumes you have read the text.

Meditate using the Weavings sections. The end of each chapter gives a Scripture verse relating to our life experience. I've also provided a quotation and questions or ideas for your meditation. Let these weavings help direct your thoughts toward God as you listen for his message to you. Be open to God's leading, not mine. Ask him questions about his Word, then sit back and listen.

Consider the prayer suggestions. In this book about prayer you'll notice there are no written prayers for you to "use," and this is intentional. I want to encourage you to move beyond the structure of "Dear God, . . . Amen" and begin to simply turn your life toward God. If prayer is a new experience for you, relax. Be yourself. God already knows you anyway. Speak to God like you talk to a friend. As he reveals himself to you (and he will), you may want to respond to him in new ways—with words of praise and worship. Don't be afraid to try something new. Open your eyes or close them, bow your head or look up, sit or kneel. Pray when you walk the dog or walk to the boardroom. Pray when you wash the dishes or the car.

Please understand, I am not advocating we give up a disciplined quiet time or prayer time. That special time set aside to meet with God is the place where we learn at his feet. There he prepares our hearts to live out his grace and gentleness in the midst of the world's hatred and roughness. It's in this place where we abide in him and he in us.

I personally spend a good portion of my morning hours reading God's Word, praying and journaling, and I plan to do so until I die. This book is one way to help you take that disciplined attitude of prayer into the rest of your life. God doesn't want just a meeting time. He wants to be by your side all the time.

Keep a journal. This will do much to help you turn your life into a prayer. Journaling slows down your mind to allow time for God to unfold your thoughts. Especially when I struggle to turn to God throughout the day, journaling allows me to regather the events of life, to spread out my thoughts and feelings onto the page and turn them again toward God. It's the best exercise I know to build a strong attitude of unceasing prayer. For your journaling experience, you can use a notebook or an actual journal.

What do you write in a journal? Anything, as long as it is directed toward God. Some days I feel like the psalmist who prayed, "The darkness is my closest friend" (Psalm 88:18). Other days I write songs of praise and joy. Don't sugarcoat your words; don't write what you think you ought to write, just write. Jot down verses you believe God is impressing on you. Write down your questions about Scripture. Record your conflicts in the workplace, or your heartache over a child struggling at school.

I think of my journal as a window to my heart. It's a tool for God to move through me. Like a gentle breeze blowing, he clears out the stale thoughts and refreshes my mind, readying me to hear his voice.

Above all, know that God delights in you every second of the day and night. No one is beyond his reach. The extent he's willing to go to be in relationship with you leads to the foot of the cross where he reveals his deepest longing to join his heart to yours at any cost. Let him weave his love into your being as your life becomes an unceasing prayer.

Part 1
UNRAVELINGS

Just when life feels "under control,"
an unexpected tugging of the heart
can unravel the most intricately woven
self-made tapestry.
But unraveling the old picture,
filled with buried pains,
prepares us for a more beautifully woven,
God-made tapestry.

❊ ❊ ❊ ❊

So after [Abraham] had been living in Canaan ten years, [Sarah] his wife took her Egyptian maidservant Hagar and gave her to her husband to be his wife. He slept with Hagar, and she conceived.

When she knew she was pregnant, she began to despise her mistress. . . .

Then [Sarah] mistreated Hagar; so she fled from her.

The angel of the LORD found Hagar near a spring in the desert; it was the spring that is beside the road to Shur. And he said, "Hagar, servant of [Sarah], where have you come from, and where are you going?"

"I'm running away from my mistress [Sarah]," she answered.

Then the angel of the LORD told her, "Go back to your mistress and submit to her." The angel added, "I will so increase your descendants that they will be too numerous to count." . . .

She gave this name to the LORD who spoke to her: "You are the God who sees me," for she said, "I have now seen the One who sees me." . . .

So Hagar bore [Abraham] a son, and [Abraham] gave the name Ishmael to the son she had borne. . . .

[Sarah] said to Abraham, "Get rid of that slave woman and her son, for that slave woman's son will never share in the inheritance with my son Isaac." . . .

Early the next morning Abraham took some food and a skin of water and gave them to Hagar. He set them on her shoulders and then sent her off with the boy. She went on her way and wandered in the desert of Beersheba.

When the water in the skin was gone, she put the boy under one of the bushes. Then she went off and sat down nearby, . . . for she thought, "I cannot watch the boy die." And as she sat there nearby, she began to sob.

God heard the boy crying and the angel of God called to Hagar from heaven and said to her, "What is the matter, Hagar? Do not be afraid; God has heard the boy crying as he lies there. . . ."

Then God opened her eyes and she saw a well of water. So she went and filled the skin with water and gave the boy a drink.

GENESIS 16:3-13, 15; 21:10-19

1

God of
the Desert

I held back the tears as long as possible. But once inside the car, I cried for several minutes, my husband patiently waiting, holding my hand. He seemed to understand that God had tugged at my heart through the sermon that morning about unresolved anger. In a matter of minutes I looked at my old wound inflicted by my ex-husband's infidelities. I recalled the day he left on a business trip and never returned until two months later to pick up some things.

Although it happened nearly fifteen years ago, and although I'd rebuilt my life with a wonderful husband and two precious daughters, the hurt felt like a freshly inflicted wound. How did I handle that pain for so many years? Not very well. Most of the time I pretended it didn't exist. I hid inside my own skin, moving through the days with a smile as my disguise.

I went through a period after the divorce when I sought attention from any man, just to prove that someone wanted me. I proved nothing except how to demolish my self-worth even further. I felt stepped on and used up emotionally, physically and spiritually. I ran hard from the pain and hid from the God of all comfort.

I learned later this was the same hard spot Hagar found herself in. Mistreated and holding a heart full of anger, she hid. She ran from her pain and literally hid in the desert. I may not have run to a desert, but that's how I felt inside — dry and lifeless. The story of Hagar came as cool water to my parched soul. There in her desert a divinely tender God came to Hagar, even though she never called to him. It was a sheer act of grace on his part.

With this tugging at my heart and these surprising tears, God came to me, even though I never called him. His grace was at work in me. My bowed head wasn't God's cue to come and listen to my problem. He knew I didn't have the strength or wisdom to call for help. My actions didn't enable him to love me. God *is* love, and God is unchangeable.

If God's own character prompted him to seek Hagar, his lost child, and begin unraveling her past hurts, then he'd do the same for me. His love called me by name, and he started a conversation with me that morning after church. God is the God of the desert and the God of dry souls.

As ugly as the anger appeared in my tapestry of life, it held together the me I'd come to be over a long period of time. I wasn't sure how to survive without it. But God's tug put me in a place where I wanted to try and where I could brace myself to hear his voice.

Unceasing prayer hears God speak first in the desert places of life.

WEAVINGS
In the same way, the Spirit helps us in our weakness. We do not know what we ought to pray for, but the Spirit himself intercedes for us with groans that words cannot express. Romans 8:26

"Prayer will quench hate, fear and panic
when nothing else will do it."
Frank Laubach, *Prayer: The Mightiest Force in the World*

❖　❖　❖　❖

Consider any areas of unresolved pain in your past. With God's grace in mind, turn those wounds toward him. Don't concern yourself with what you should do about it or say about it. Just rest in his love and his desire to be in an intimate relationship with you.

2

Going Back Again

"Why is Mommy crying?" my four-year-old daughter asked her daddy from the car seat in back.

Knowing I had more crying to do, he answered, "I think Mommy's crying 'cause she's angry about something."

"Angry at me?" she asked quickly.

"No," my husband assured. "Mommy forgot to talk to somebody about some problems. She kept her feelings inside too long." With a little smile to relieve the tension, he added with great fatherly wisdom, "You know if you keep your feelings inside, they get rotten and make you feel sad."

Our daughter nodded her head in all seriousness. This time, talking to me, she said, "Why are you angry, Mommy?" Her words cut straight to my heart, and I knew God was using the innocent voice of my child to ask the hard question, "Why are you angry?"

Throughout Scripture God asks tough questions. When Adam and Eve hid in shame in the Garden of Eden, God asked, "Where are you?" To a murderous Cain, he asked, "Where is your brother? What have you done?" To Job he said, "Brace yourself . . . I will question you and you shall answer me." (Job 40:7). God asked Hagar some tough questions too when he came to her in the desert: "Where have you come from, and where are you going?"

So in the days and weeks to follow I "braced myself" to explore how I would answer God. At first, I muddled through my list of justified excuses: "I'm angry because my ex-husband lied and cheated . . . because I didn't have the emotional strength to confront him when I should have . . . because I gave him my best and it wasn't good enough . . . because, because, because."

But still, I felt a continued tug unraveling the excuses until the truth stood naked between me and God: I was angry because I needed a weapon—a weapon for keeping others, including God, at arm's length, ensuring I'd never be hurt again. It gave me an instrument to manipulate others and to attempt to control my world.

At the end of that unraveled thread, God showed me my bandaged heart. I knew he wanted the layers of bandaging pulled away to reveal the damage inflicted by my own anger. It wasn't a pretty sight. I had become a withdrawn, silent, uncommunicative woman, with a dwindling number of friends and shaky family relationships.

I knew the outcome of my relationship with God was dependent on the choice I made at this point. Would I continue hiding and ignoring the sin and pain, hoping God wouldn't notice? Or would I humble myself in obedience and acknowledge God as the One who can do all things? Could I choose, as Hagar did, to return to God and to enjoy a growing relationship with "the One who sees me."

So I came to God and confessed my sin, agreeing with him that I had misused my anger. I sought his mercy for the times I had failed to put that emotion into his hands. I had appointed myself lord over my anger for too long.

Next I asked my husband to forgive me for bringing that bitterness into our marriage relationship, for mistrusting him without reason. Because of my anger and pain, I had sown distrust into our relationship without cause.

Finally, God tugged again, encouraging me to confess my anger and my sin to Christian friends, to allow the body of Christ to bear some of my burden and to minister to my hurting heart. So, for the first time, I revealed to three other people how hurt I had been over that part of my life and how bitter I'd become through the years. I removed the armor, put down the weapon and unbandaged the wound. And I didn't fall apart. God's grace was sufficient to see me through. His touch was sufficient to heal. His love was sufficient to remove bitterness. His sacrifice was sufficient to wash away sin.

"Where have you come from?" This question that God asked Hagar reminds me there is a time to look back at past pains, to look at where I've come from. And as I do, he wants me to turn it all toward him.

"And where are you going?" There is also a time to move ahead, to leave the desert and the unraveled tapestry and bandages and determine the next step forward. I wasn't sure where I was going, but I chose to go with God. It was time to let him begin to recraft my life into one pleasing to him.

Unceasing prayer answers the hard questions and lets God recraft past pains.

WEAVINGS
Forget the former things; do not dwell on the past.
See, I am doing a new thing! Now it springs up; do you not perceive it?
I am making a way in the desert and streams in the wasteland . . .
to give drink to my people, my chosen, the people I formed for myself
that they may proclaim my praise. Isaiah 43:18-20

"The sweet language of experience is 'Thou God seest me.' When the eyes of the soul looking out meet the eyes of God looking in, heaven has begun right here on this earth."
A.W. Tozer, *The Pursuit of God*

❊   ❊   ❊   ❊

In looking at the past pain you identified in chapter one, what question does God ask of you? Have you wrestled through the tough questions? Ask him to show you the areas where you maintain lordship rather than letting him recraft the past. What specific action does he want you to take now?

3

Emptiness

For several weeks after my "confessions," my spirit soared. I laughed more than I had in years. I called people when I normally would have kept to myself. God, family and friends literally loved me out of my desert. That's why I was shocked one day when my old withdrawn and angry self crept back inside me, looking for a place to call home. Worry about relationships often overwhelmed me.

"Where were you?" I asked my husband when he arrived home a half hour late from work.

"I picked up the dry cleaning. Why? Do we need to be somewhere?" he asked, holding a plastic-wrapped suit on a hanger.

"Why didn't you call and tell me?" I launched into interrogation mode, wondering in the back of my mind if he was thinking about leaving me too. Such conversations and paranoid thoughts plagued me. God and I had worked hard to unravel that picture. But in the months that followed, the old scene restitched itself into a dark tapestry of fear. Disappointment shrouded my heart when I realized the unraveling wasn't the complete, one-time healing I'd hoped for.

After following all that thread back to my first stitch of anger, and after following God's lead out of the desert into his lush garden of comfort, I expected to be done with this pain. Hagar also had answered the hard questions and retraced her steps. She even returned to her position as Sarah's servant and lived there, along with her son Ishmael, for fourteen years. But meeting God in the desert and obeying his command didn't pave a smooth path for her.

In fact, the old rivalry didn't die.

After Sarah finally gave birth to her own son, Isaac, the animosity between these women became unbearable, resulting in Abraham sending Hagar and Ishmael packing back to the desert. Her disappointment must have weighed heavier than the skin of water and food she carried on her shoulders. Was this what Hagar expected out of a life submitted to God's will?

I too felt burdened by the hurt and anger that sometimes boiled inside me, shutting down my emotions and calling me to withdraw again to the desert places of my heart. It's not easy to acknowledge God's goodness when things aren't going the way I expect. Now, like Hagar, I was at the end of my resources. How much longer could I rely on my own will or intelligence or personality to keep me out of the desert? How far could an old encounter with God take me? About as far as it took Hagar, because past experience, even with God, doesn't fill my need for him today.

The water had run dry long ago. Listening to her son's cry of thirst, Hagar kept a distant deathwatch from a nearby bush. Eventually sobs wracked her body as she witnessed the horror of her child dying a torturously slow death. But God did not forget his promises. He came to Hagar again. There was one last step in this healing process. God wanted her emptiness.

When I get to a place where I can't pray because my hope, my strength or my faith has run dry, God asks me to turn over the emptiness to him. He's always looking for an empty vessel to fill with his presence. But he doesn't just take my empty bottle and refill it. He throws away the bottle. That's the frightening part—to trust him enough to throw away my self-sufficiency because he wants to give me something better.

When Hagar saw God come near to her again, he opened her eyes and she saw just a few steps away not a new skin of water, but something much better. She saw God's deep well waiting to quench her thirst and save her son. Just when I think I'm running on empty . . . just when I feel disappointed with unexpected feelings or circumstances . . . just when I've reached the end of my resources . . . God leads me to his deep well of love and sufficiency.

Sometimes God's healing and the changes he makes in me are fast and immediate. But more often it's slow and ongoing, like unceasing prayer. It's not in my asking and receiving a quick, miraculous answer that my faith grows stronger. It's what lies in between. It's in the waiting and persevering where I learn to rely on him by emptying myself. In fact, there's no need to wait until I'm at the end of my rope. If I freely pour out my self-sufficiency each day, God opens my eyes to his sweet water of life. It's been there all along, lying just beyond my fears.

Unceasing prayer turns an empty heart to God,
who turns it into a new vessel overflowing with his deep love.

WEAVINGS
And I am convinced and sure of this very thing, that He who began
a good work in you will continue until the day of Jesus Christ
right up to the time of his return developing that good work and
perfecting and bringing it to full completion in you.
PHILIPPIANS 1:6 AMPLIFIED.

"You cannot stay where you are and go with God."
Henry Blackaby, *Experiencing God*

❀   ❀   ❀   ❀

What attitude or misconception about your desert place does God want to reshape? Are you willing to trust in his goodness regardless of the outcome? When you offer God the empty bottle of your self-sufficiency, how does he replace it? When he opens your eyes to his presence, what do you see?

Part 2

THE WEAVER

A tapestry reflects the heart of the weaver.
Honoring God's mastery means recognizing
his work and wisdom, even as he weaves
the coarse fiber into our lives.

❋   ❋   ❋   ❋

*Isaac prayed to the L*ORD *on behalf of his wife, because she was barren. The L*ORD
*answered his prayer, and his wife Rebekah became pregnant. The babies jostled each
other within her, and she said, "Why is this happening to me?" So she went to inquire
of the L*ORD

*The L*ORD *said to her, "Two nations are in your womb, and two peoples from within
you will be separated; one people will be stronger than the other, and the older will
serve the younger." . . .*

*Now there was a famine in the land—besides the earlier famine of Abraham's
time—and Isaac went to Abimelech king of the Philistines in Gerar. The L*ORD
*appeared to Isaac and said, "Do not go down to Egypt; live in the land where I tell
you to live. Stay in this land for a while, and I will be with you and will bless you.
For to you and your descendants I will give all these lands and will confirm the oath
I swore to your father Abraham.*

GENESIS 25:21-23; 26:1-3

4

Why Ask Why?

"Okay, take a breath and hold it."

A click, a hum and another click later, I breathed, glad to be done with the mammogram. I pulled the gown back over my shoulder.

"Wait here, please," the technician said as she exited the room. It gave me time to think about all these machines and advances in medicine. If they had been in place forty years ago, no doubt they would have saved my grandmother's life.

Several minutes later, the woman knocked and opened the door. "The radiologist wants another couple of shots if you don't mind." She smiled apologetically.

"Why?" The question blurted out of my mouth with a tinge of panic.

"You didn't smile," she joked, trying to put my mind at ease. But my gut told me this wasn't the end of it.

I wasn't surprised when my doctor called two days later to schedule a consultation regarding the mammogram. Two spots . . . lumps . . . had been detected in my right breast and needed to be removed. He referred me to a surgeon who scheduled me for out-patient surgery three weeks later—just enough time to really panic.

Again I asked, "Why?" This time to God. "Why do I have to wait three weeks? Why do I have to stare at the possibility of cancer and death when I'm only thirty-seven years old with a husband and two daughters depending on me? Why, Lord?"

It wasn't like me to question God's timing. I wanted to believe my faith was beyond the need to ask "why." I should be able to trust his purpose, even when I didn't see the way or the reason. Wasn't this the part where I was supposed to consider it a joy when I face all kinds of trials? (James 1:2). I guess I had some growing to do because I just wasn't there yet.

Rebekah prayed such a prayer too. Through her simple, honest question, God began to teach me how to pray through the conflicts that jostle my spirit. Her conflict wasn't extraordinary, but all the same, it brought her to the point of asking God, "Why is this happening to me?" Her circumstance was as natural as having a baby. In fact, her pregnancy was a direct answer to prayer. Even so, the jostling inside her created unexpected conflict.

In the original Hebrew language, to "inquire of God" meant to follow or pursue God—to worship him by diligently seeking him. That idea derailed my guilt trip about questioning God. In fact, he must want me to ask him "why" in every circumstance of life. By doing so, I honor his authority over me, and it gives him the opportunity to reveal his purposes. Such worship tells him I completely trust his ability to create beauty in his tapestry, even when I feel only the coarseness of the fiber.

Was I really seeking him, or merely seeking comfort and relief from this hardship? I wasn't sure my motives for asking "why" grew out of my desire to worship him. Inquiring of God was the first step to praying through those conflicts that jostle inside me.

Unceasing prayer isn't afraid to ask God "why."

WEAVINGS
Why are you downcast, O my soul? Why so disturbed within me?
Put your hope in God, for I will yet praise him, my Savior and my God.
PSALM 42:5

"[God] made you and He therefore understands you, and knows
how to manage you, and you must therefore trust Him to do it."
Hannah W. Smith, *The Christian's Secret of a Happy Life*

❧   ❧   ❧   ❧

Describe or consider a situation when you wanted to ask God why
something was happening. How do you feel about asking God "why"?
Tell him about that feeling.

5

Motives

The news of the impending surgery and the wait became more than
I could handle. Every day I called the surgeon's office and asked the
receptionist, "Did anyone cancel their surgery? Did any dates open
up on the doctor's calendar?" This need to control and the need to
know the outcome of my conflict burdened everyone, including that
poor receptionist. Each night in bed I cried like a baby; frustration
heaped upon frustration impacted my heart with fear, infecting my
soul with doubts about God's goodness.

More afraid than I'd ever been of what the future held, I continued to wonder, "Why?" And the more I asked, the more I wondered,
"*Why* won't you answer me, God?" I just didn't seem to be getting
through to him. No response, no miracle cure, no open appoint-
ments. And the more I wondered, the more my question echoed back
to me from heaven, "Why? Why do you need to know the details of
the future? What's your motive?"

In that echo, my "why" whined in self-pity and left no room for a listening heart. I had asked God a question, but I really didn't want to hear his answer. I harbored the kind of fear that reasons, "If I tell God I'm all his, he might send me to a mission camp in the jungles of India. Or, he might ask me to *die* for him."

After the birth of their sons, Isaac and Rebekah faced another dilemma. Isaac tried to solve the problem of living through a famine. As Isaac negotiated his own solution, God told him he had other plans. "Do not go down to Egypt," he said to Isaac. "Live in the land where I tell you to live. Stay in this land for a while, and I will be with you and will bless you" (Genesis 26:2-3). Those words shocked me as I happened to read them one morning in the midst of this conflict. Was that his message for me? Was I to live with this conflict jostling inside me? Maybe in this dilemma he wanted me to learn to lean on him.

So I began to weed out my impure motives. Was I doubting God's goodness or proving it? Was I confirming his purpose or confounding it? Was I worshiping my Lord or rebelling against his authority? If I'm limiting his authority over me, then I'm insulting his sovereignty over his creation. I'm putting him into my own little God-shaped box where I try to control him, making him fit my reality, and telling him, "This is the way you should be."

I expect him to behave in certain ways inside the box of my life, and then I close the lid tight, insuring that no unexpected turn of events escapes. When I try to control God, I fail the motive test. I'm doubting his ability to be in control. I'm confounding his good purposes by replacing them with my own, and I'm rebelling against his lordship.

My first step, before asking one more question, was to confess my sin to God. I had, indeed, used my selfish desire for comfort as my motive for inquiring of God. I had used the facade of righteous inquiry to mask my fears. But just as I repented, God did an amazing thing. He met me in that box I had built—not so that I could confine him there—so that he could escort me out into a spacious place.

He wants my relationship with him to be bigger and broader. He wants it to expand far, far beyond the constraints of my self-imposed walls. Opening the lid to my box, I was ready to begin again. This time with a pure heart, I asked, "Why, Lord?"

Unceasing prayer recognizes God's authority and goodness.

WEAVINGS

I am the LORD your God, who teaches you what is best for you,
who directs you in the way you should go.
If only you had paid attention to my commands,
your peace would have been like a river,
your righteousness like the waves of the sea. ISAIAH 48:17-18

"To begin to comprehend that God is at work weaving the events of our lives for our welfare is essential for my trust in Him."
Cynthia Heald, *Becoming a Woman of Purpose*

❖   ❖   ❖   ❖

Be honest with God about your motives for asking him "why." He wants you to ask him the hard questions, and he won't be surprised by them. Ask him to use your questions to draw you closer to him.

6

Worship

For years I assumed good Christians didn't ask God "why." We simply accepted the hard knocks of life in faith. But when his children ask him "Why?" for the umpteenth time, God isn't a short-tempered parent who snaps, "Because I said so," or "That's just the way it is." God wants to answer and reveal himself, just as he answered Rebekah's inquiry. Her why-prayer sought to understand God in the midst of her conflict. But his response surprised me.

Actually I was surprised most of all by what God didn't say. He didn't remove her discomfort. Neither did he outline the ultimate reason for the conflict, or paint a false picture of a bright future. But, his answer did uncover the truth of her condition. (Remember, they didn't have ultrasound back then. This was possibly the first she knew she would give birth to twins.) He also prepared her to deal with future conflicts between her children. Finally, he reaffirmed his promise and his purpose by stating, "Two *nations* are in your womb." This was the promise given to Abraham, Rebekah's father-in-law, to become a great nation and God's chosen people.

After getting over my guilt trip of asking God "why," I was quick to note Rebekah didn't continue to whine and question God. She presented her question as a prayer, an act of worship, a means of seeking and intimately knowing him. To be honest, when I ask God "why," I'm often asking for deliverance rather than strength to endure. It was time to start seeing God's goodness in the midst of this conflict as the simple answer to my prayer.

There's another in Scripture who asked God "why." At the end of his life, Jesus gave a piercing cry from the cross, "My God, My God, *why* have you forsaken me?" (Matthew 27:46). Jesus' pure motive trusted God's goodness for the outcome. That little word *why* in both the Old and New Testaments means "For what good?" It's asking for a demonstration of an idea or purpose. On the cross, Jesus asked his Father, "For what good are you forsaking me? What idea are you demonstrating? What will result from your forsaking me?"

I remembered how clearly Jesus had seen the whole plan of redemption just days, even hours, before the cross. I remembered how beautifully he comforted his disciples and prayed for them in the upper room (John 14–17). But now Jesus seemed to be searching for God's will. He wanted to know God's reasons for the conflict jostling inside him.

There in his final moment, with the full weight of our sin separating him from God, Jesus best understood what life is like for us. He saw why we struggle to discern God's will, why we question and sometimes seem lost in finding our way to him. Jesus' death required him to search, just as I search, to understand God in relation to his conflict. There on the cross, in the center of his pain, he worshiped God with his question, "Why?"

So I asked God again. "Why? Why do I need to go through this medical ordeal?" As with Rebekah, he didn't remove my discomfort or insure a bright future. But he revealed the truth about my condition—not physically, but spiritually—how my fears lead me to distrust his goodness. He prepared me to expect conflict in days to come, and he confirmed his promise to never leave me or forsake me. And that was enough.

I survived the three-week wait. After being poked by more needles than I ever want to see again, I came through it. Two lumps were removed, both benign. But I was left with a living, growing faith that allows me to ask "why." And when I take time to ask in prayer, to turn those struggles toward God, he lets me see just a little more clearly how to embrace his goodness in the midst of my conflicts. I was ready to stop wrestling the Great Weaver and start trusting his handiwork in my life.

Unceasing prayer longs for God in the midst of conflict.

WEAVINGS
For our light and momentary troubles are achieving for us
an eternal glory that far outweighs them all. 2 CORINTHIANS *4:17*

"Sometimes when we ask God our Why questions, instead
of giving us answers, he gives us himself."
Mary Jane Worden, quoted in *Rainbow of Hope,* comp.
Billy Hughey and Janice Hughey.

❊   ❊   ❊   ❊

Today, what are the biggest or most frequent conflicts that arise in your life? Write down any question you've been holding back from God. Ask as many questions as you want, or one big question you've been afraid to ask. Now, be still before God, and listen to him. Let him reveal himself as you honor and worship him in your inquiry.

Part 3

THE WARP
THREADS

The warp threads anchor a tapestry like
a canvas anchors paint, but it requires stretching
and restretching the fibers to create a smooth picture.
The peaks and valleys of life may look like wrinkles
in the tapestry, but God works in us to stretch and
smooth our spirits, until we learn to rest in
the contentment of belonging to him.

❊   ❊   ❊   ❊

*When Pharaoh's horses, chariots and horsemen went into the sea, the LORD
brought the waters of the sea back over them, but the Israelites walked through
the sea on dry ground. Then Miriam the prophetess, Aaron's sister, took a
tambourine in her hand, and all the women followed her, with tambourines and
dancing. Miriam sang to them: "Sing to the LORD, for he is highly exalted. The
horse and its rider he has hurled into the sea."*

*Then Moses led Israel from the Red Sea and they went into the Desert of Shur.
For three days they traveled in the desert without finding water. When they came to
Marah, they could not drink its water because it was bitter. (That is why the place
is called Marah.) So the people grumbled against Moses, saying, "What are we to
drink?"*

*Then Moses cried out to the LORD, and the LORD showed him a piece of wood. He
threw it into the water, and the water became sweet.*

EXODUS 15:19-25

7

The Furthest Thing
from My Mind

"You look happy." My husband smiled as he knotted his blue silk necktie.

I stopped my humming long enough to smile back at him. We wrapped our arms around each other and shared the victory of this morning. It marked my first day on the job as a full-time wife and mom. Homemade pancakes topped my to-do list.

The clanging pot and sizzling griddle seemed to sing along with me. Today blue jeans triumphed over pantyhose, pancake batter claimed victory over frozen waffles, and mommy's hugs lasted all day long instead of just in the morning and evening. Ready to enter my Promised Land, we celebrated this long-awaited victory.

Since the birth of our daughter, my heart was never on my job. It always beat for hearth and home. But we weren't naive as we considered the financial risks. Still we felt God paving the path, providing dry ground for us to walk on as he rolled back the sea of objections that had stopped us from making this change earlier. It meant major lifestyle adjustments. Above and beyond the obvious loss of my income, we became a one-car family. We changed our eat-out-every-other-night routine to a twice-a-month coupon-sponsored date.

Miriam, Moses' sister, knew what a change in lifestyle meant too. She, along with the entire nation of Israel, had just pulled up her enslaved roots from Egyptian soil and, with God's blessing, said,

"This is the day we set off to claim our own Promised Land from God." He paved their path to freedom, providing dry ground for them to walk on as he literally rolled back a wet sea in their path. When he swept the sea back over the pursuing Egyptian army, he effectively washed away their last tie to slavery.

Following that victory, the entire nation celebrated with a party unequaled in all of history. By my estimation, Miriam and the other Israelite women numbered in the hundreds of thousands, all singing and dancing and playing tambourines. Scarves and skirts swirling, gold bangles and baubles flashing, laughing, shouting, more singing, dancing, "Sing to the LORD, for he is highly exalted. The horse and the rider he has hurled into the sea." (Exodus 15:21). What a sight! What a victory!

That triumph stretched their faith like the warp threads on a tapestry loom. It propelled them into new heights with God. Their victory magnified God's glory, while he increased their joy in him. That's the feeling I embraced as I made this change in my life. In fact, if it hadn't been for our need to save money in every creative way possible, I would have tossed out the box of frozen toaster waffles that said, "Hot on your plate in minutes!" After all, I was a homemaker now, and I could home-make my waffles if I pleased.

Hardship and challenges were the furthest thing from my mind, and well they should have been. I had no regrets about my decision, no guilt about staying home. Blue jeans, pancakes and hugs won the battle this day, and we rejoiced in God's goodness with stacks of hotcakes loaded with butter and sweet syrup.

Unceasing prayer celebrates the victories.

WEAVINGS
Thanks be to God, who in Christ always leads us in triumph
(as trophies of Christ's victory). 2 CORINTHIANS 2:14 AMPLIFIED

> "Now and then it's good to pause
> in our pursuit of happiness and just be happy."
> Anonymous, quoted in *Rainbow of Hope*,
> comp. Billy Hughey and Janice Hughey.

❈ ❈ ❈ ❈

Consider some of the "victories" in your life. How did you celebrate? Were you aware of God's presence in the victory? Ask God to show you how he has used those times to stretch your faith, or to prepare you for another experience.

8

After the Party

"This is why I wanted to stay home?" I sarcastically wondered. Then, addressing my three-year-old daughter, I asked, "Why did you put the hairbrush in the potty?" Sitting uncomfortably on the tiled floor, my arm half immersed in the toilet, I fished out the brush she "accidentally" tossed in.

"I need to see if it goes in the hole," she explained with childlike candor.

"I've told you before, things don't go in the hole," I argued emphatically. "If it does go down the hole, the potty won't work." After retrieving my hairbrush from its watery near-death experience, I tossed it into the trash and sent my daughter to her room for a "time out." I was honest enough to tell her, "Mommy needs some time out too."

This new role of full-time mom and official homebody wasn't what

I had expected. Just a few short months ago I handily managed a dozen adults in a busy office. Now at home I stood toe-to-toe with a single strong-willed three-year-old whom I couldn't seem to wrangle into bed for a catnap! Was I the same woman who had developed time-saving processes and new systems for a Fortune 500 company? Why couldn't I keep a kitchen drawer filled with clean silverware for more than a day?

"So this is what it feels like when the party's over," I mumbled to myself. I sat with a cup of tea and vaguely remembered that victory celebration. I already felt fed up and trapped, and then I felt guilty for thinking it. I wanted out. "Was this all a mistake, God? Did I misunderstand your leading or your timing for me to be at home?"

The same feelings crept into the Israelites after that miraculous Red Sea victory and Miriam's party to beat all parties. Maybe these thoughts weren't so unusual after a triumphant experience. Stepping just beyond the Red Sea, I hear the first rumblings of discontentment in the people of Israel.

Their grumbling stood directly opposed to the song of triumph. So why do the two extremes always seem to show up together? The Israelites were in the midst of the ordinary tasks of living—like looking for water—when they got caught complaining and grumbling. I don't think it was the water so much as their state of mind that made everything taste bitter. After the Red Sea, everything else looked and tasted like unsweetened lemonade. Their grumbling gave voice to their spirit of discontent not only with their circumstances, but with God.

Finding victory in the ordinary routines of life was like looking for water in the desert . . . or a hairbrush in the commode. I was living in the desert, and the water tasted bitter. I wasn't asking God for a big Red Sea miracle. I'd be happy with a ripple in the toilet water. But that was still grumbling, and all I could do was turn to God in spite of the bitter-tasting water, and let him do his work in my life.

Unceasing prayer looks to God in spite of bitter waters.

WEAVINGS
Do everything without complaining. PHILIPPIANS 2:14

"The Lord wants to give us the raw courage to face life
as it is and receive power to change it,
beginning with ourselves. Don't leave the battle.
Your post of duty was elected for you,
and there you will find more of God than you'll find in
a self-imposed exile of escape.
He's there in the battle with you!"
Lloyd John Ogilvie, *Falling into Greatness*

❁   ❁   ❁   ❁

What routines in your daily life do you wish you could change? Is there
anything about which you often complain? Turn your complaint into
an opportunity to ask God for his vision in this situation.

9

Finding
the Victory

I love sarcastic humor. But I'm not sure God found it amusing when
I asked him, "Now, which part of my routine am I supposed to find
victorious today? Is it listening to the Barney video for the eighth
time before noon? Is it my daughter's tantrum over being served
soup instead of cereal for lunch? Is it the challenge of trying to make

a diaper pail smell like something other than a diaper pail?"

Time to stretch the threads. My grumbling had pressed deep wrinkles into the fiber God had prepared for my tapestry. I wasn't *unwilling* to sing the victory song the way Miriam did after crossing the Red Sea. It's just that most days I couldn't *see* the victory in my ordinary life. But the story of Miriam and the Israelites journeying in the desert continued to plant ideas in my mind. That Hebrew crowd found it difficult to sing a victory song as they marched through the desert without water. Even when God led them to the water, it tasted bitter.

Maybe their prayers, like mine, took on a sarcastic bite. "Now, which part of this picture are we supposed to find victorious, God? Is it this beautiful scenery full of sand, rocks and thorns? Is it the fact that we're all enjoying this family camp out? Or is it this lovely provision of water before us which makes us happy to be thirsty rather than swallow the bitter stuff?"

I think we were both missing the point as well as the victory. After all this grumbling, God showed Moses something unusual, but something full of beautiful symbolism. Exodus 15:25 says, "The LORD showed him a piece of wood. He threw it into the water, and the water became sweet." God offered a piece of wood — not the miracle-working staff of Aaron, not a mighty tree or rock to strike allowing sweet water to pour forth. It was a plain piece of wood, a stick. Maybe he even stubbed his toe on it. But whatever happened, Moses realized it was from God, and he tossed it into the bitter water, turning it sweet.

Just like a parent with a child, God offered simple instructions, as they turned their eyes from their own grumbling and toward him: "Listen carefully . . . do what is right . . . pay attention . . . keep [my] decrees" (v. 26). Moses took the simple object at his feet and gave it to God, and God blessed them with his presence and his direction.

So I tried it too. I thanked him for the Barney video, tossing it like a stick of wood into my bitterness. I let him have that stinky diaper pail and sincerely asked, "What do you want me to learn here?" Each day I found even the tiniest evidence of his presence in my wilderness and thanked him for it. With these tiny sticks of praise

God sent sweet water and heavenly manna into my journey with him. I thanked him for the breath of life I heard in the tiny snore of my sleeping child. I grasped the excitement of discovering the wonders of this world with my daughter as she screamed at finding a big black bug or laughed at the leaves racing each other down a windy street

It wasn't much, and God didn't always give deep spiritual revelations. But it was enough to turn my focus off me and toward the Giver of every good and perfect gift. In my ordinary routines I have a choice, and that in itself is reason to celebrate. God created me with a free will. I can choose to grumble my way through life or to rise up in victory. God placed enough sticks of wood in my path to sweeten the routine waters of life with joy and delight.

Sometimes I fight against God when he wants to stretch my faith. But he's smoothing out my wrinkled spirit as I learn to rest in the sweet contentment of being his child.

Unceasing prayer finds God's glory in ordinary moments of life.

WEAVINGS
I have learned the secret of being content in any and every situation. . . .
I can do everything through him who gives me strength.
PHILIPPIANS 4:12-13

"Healthy prayer necessitates frequent experiences of the common, earthy, run-of-the mill variety. Like walks, and talks, and good wholesome laughter. Like work in the yard, and chitchat with neighbors, and washing windows. Like loving our spouse, and playing with our kids, and working with our colleagues.
Richard Foster, *Prayer: Finding the Heart's True Home*

❊　❊　❊　❊

What makes you feel defeated rather than victorious in Christ? Ask God to give you a new vision of his goodness. Finish this prayer thought: *I praise you, Lord, because . . .*

Part 4
THE LOOM

Like the wooden loom surrounding and supporting
the tapestry, God surrounds us with
a great cloud of witnesses: godly men and women
to wrap their arms around us and hold us tight
in loving accountability to his ways.

❉   ❉   ❉   ❉

*The Israelites once again did evil in the eyes of the Lord. So the Lord sold them
into the hands of Jabin, a king of Canaan. . . . The commander of his army was
Sisera. . . . Because he had nine hundred iron chariots and had cruelly oppressed
the Israelites for twenty years, [the Israelites] cried to the Lord for help.*

*Deborah, a prophetess, . . . was leading Israel at that time. She held court under
the Palm of Deborah. . . . She sent for Barak . . . and said to him, "The Lord, the
God of Israel, commands you: 'Go, take with you ten thousand men of Naphtali
and Zebulun and lead the way to Mount Tabor. I will lure Sisera . . . with his chariots
and his troops to the Kishon River and give him into your hands.'"*

*Barak said to her, "If you go with me, I will go; but if you don't go with me, I won't
go."*

*"Very well," Deborah said, "I will go with you. But because of the way you are going
about this, the honor will not be yours, for the Lord will hand Sisera over to a woman."
So Deborah went with Barak to Kedesh, where he summoned Zebulun and Naphtali.
Ten thousand men followed him, and Deborah also went with him. . . .*

*Then Deborah said to Barak, "Go! This is the day the Lord has given Sisera
into your hands. Has not the Lord gone ahead of you?" So Barak went down Mount
Tabor, followed by ten thousand men. . . .*

On that day God subdued Jabin, the Canaanite king, before the Israelites. . . .

On that day Deborah and Barak son of Abinoam sang this song:

"Wake up, wake up, Deborah!
 Wake up, wake up, break out in song!
Arise, O Barak!
 Take captive your captives. . . .

"In the districts of Reuben there was much searching of heart.
 Gilead stayed beyond the Jordan.
  And Dan, why did he linger by the ships?
Asher remained on the coast and stayed in his coves.

"The people of Zebulun risked their very lives;
 so did Naphtali on the heights of the field. . . .

"March on, my soul; be strong! . . .

"May they who love you be like the sun
 when it rises in its strength."
      J U D G E S 4:1-10, 14, 23; 5:1, 12, 16-18, 21, 31

10

Surprising Loneliness

As my daughters started elementary school and made new friends, they began to ask me, "Who's your best friend, Mommy?" I used to answer such questions with, "Daddy, of course." But now they responded, "No, you can't count your family. It has to be a friend." That's when I realized that other than family members, I had no close friends—no one I regularly called to share a funny story, to meet for lunch or to pray with over a problem.

This achy loneliness surprised me. By nature I'm an introvert. I like to be alone. I may be the original Lone Ranger Christian. I remember as an eleven-year-old deciding I wanted to accept Christ as my Savior. So one Sunday, when the pastor gave an invitation at the end of a service, I marched down the aisle taking my stand for Jesus. But I wondered why my parents looked so surprised.

"We're so happy about your decision," my dad said as he hugged me, "but we didn't know you were thinking about it. Didn't you want to talk to us about it?" I shrugged my shoulders, wondering why I needed to talk to anyone, my parents included, about something so personal. I don't like to ask for help—not even from God sometimes. But I was one of those kids who couldn't figure out why the Lone Ranger needed Tonto to ride beside him and help him out in a pinch. Maybe that's why the story of Deborah, in the book of Judges, fascinates me.

In a sense, Deborah was a Lone Ranger. The only woman to hold the position of Ruling Judge in Israel, she had a personal connection to God and spoke as his prophetess. My guess is she wasn't the first choice for a best friend. But after talking to God one day and receiving his directions, she obeyed, and called on another to accomplish the work God had begun in her.

She called on a man named Barak, and they learned to rely on each other, to be vulnerable in their midst of weakness, bold in the midst of battle and loyal in the midst of challenge. Deborah may not have been looking for a friendship, but she accepted the gift of friendship God brought to her. They honored God in victory and together celebrated by singing a song—a musical prayer.

That's what I longed for. Someone to say, "How can I help you hear God's voice?" I longed for someone to work with me shoulder to shoulder, someone to hold me accountable while providing encouragement and someone I could encourage as well. So I began to ask God to help me find a good friend—another God-loving woman to walk alongside me in my spiritual journey. I didn't need or want this person to take the place of God, but rather to join him and me as we all worked together.

I think God likes it that way. He demonstrated his approval of friendships through the stories of Jonathan and David, Paul and Barnabas, Mary and Elizabeth. Adam wasn't complete without Eve. And even Jesus called on others to help him fulfill his ministry. I knew God understood my desire for friendship. I knew he would answer my prayer in time. But I also knew a deep friendship wouldn't just land in my lap. It would require effort and time on my part to cultivate a treasured relationship.

Meanwhile I would let Deborah and Barak guide my thoughts as I remained on the lookout for that special someone I could call "my best friend."

Unceasing prayer lets God build and bless friendships to fulfill his plans.

"Best friend, my well-spring in the wilderness."
George Eliot, *The Spanish Gypsy*

❖   ❖   ❖   ❖

If you don't have a good friend, ask God to direct you to one and show you how to develop the relationship. If you do have a best friend, ask God to teach you what it means to him to be a friend and to have a friend.

11

Taking Risks

"I'm so nervous about teaching this workshop," I confessed to my husband as I gathered my notes for a women's conference at a local church.

"Remember, if you aren't living on the edge you're taking up too much space." His life motto was an easy one for him to live up to. He's a risk taker in every sense of the word. Not reckless, mind you, but willing to stand on the edge of a new challenge day after day and trust God to take him through it. He starts new businesses for the fun of it. He makes friends with anyone who crosses his path. He

addresses large gatherings of business leaders and government offi-
cials without even a note card in his hand.

I asked him once, "Aren't you ever nervous or afraid?" He responded
by swaggering around the room, hands on his hips, ready to draw his
guns, and taught me the lesson he learned from Marshall Matt Dillon
on "Gunsmoke." "Son," he said, "the man who's never afraid is a fool."

"I guess that must make me one of the wisest women in town," I
countered as I contemplated the fears I battled during a given day.
I'm not a risk taker. I'm a safety maker. The riskiest thing I do some
days is delete a sentence I just wrote. If I'm feeling really daring, I
might rearrange paragraphs of my writing, praying I haven't hope-
lessly ruined my chances for a Pulitzer Prize.

It's my Lone Ranger syndrome that makes me happy to be alone
with my words. But during the past several months, I felt God calling
me away from my safety zone—nine-square-feet in front of my
computer. It's easy to hide behind written words or a computer
screen. It's more difficult to come out face to face and say, "This is
what I mean by my words, and this is what I've learned. This is how
God deals with me."

So I made a plan and began writing letters to a few women in
church ministry and said, "I'd like to speak to your group." My
husband thought I was off my rocker. He knew how unlike me this
was. But God had planted the desire in my heart, and there was no
ignoring it. As soon as I stepped forward with a plan in faith, God
opened the doors. And as I began taking new risks in faith, I also felt
the need to pray for strong friendships.

Barak was ready to take a step of faith, but there's no denying he
had fears as well. That's when Deborah approached him and encouraged him to move forward, one step at a time. They stood together
in this test of faith, and they sang about the resulting victory: "The
people of Zebulun risked their very lives; so did Naphtali on the
heights of the field" (v. 18). In battle, if someone stands on the heights
of the field, they fight in the most vulnerable, visible position. Those
words reminded me of where I needed to be.

Moving out from behind my computer into the open space of friendships made me feel vulnerable. And leaving a keyboard to grasp a podium turned my steady hands into shaking symbols of my weakness. I would have to trust Christ's assurance when he said that in weakness his strength would shine through (2 Corinthians 12:9-10). Now, more than ever, I needed outside support and prayer warriors because as opportunities to teach or speak came up, I was the one wondering if I was off my rocker for saying yes.

I don't want to be like the Israelites in Deborah's song who took cover on the coasts and in the coves when it came time to fight. I may be afraid, but courage doesn't mean having no fear. It means I walk through the challenge and take action despite the fear. And that's when I need a friend the most.

Unceasing prayer takes faith to the edge of fear and jumps into God's arms.

WEAVINGS
And one standing alone can be attacked and defeated, but two can stand back-to-back and conquer; three is even better, for a triple-braided cord is not easily broken. ECCLESIASTES *4:12 TLB*

"However much my love-meeting is God-and-I,
it is also God-and-you-and-I. For the more God's love flows
into me, the more that love crests and builds to a torrent in
me that flows over into you. And that same powerful love runs
among us and we are held together in a current of joy."
Emilie Griffin, *Clinging*

❈　　❈　　❈　　❈

What do you think you could accomplish if you had a good friend to encourage you and no other obstacles (financial or otherwise)? Present that dream or desire to God for his approval, then take steps of faith as he leads.

12

Encouraging Each Other

The call was unexpected, but not a coincidence of fate. I recognized God's open door to friendship when I saw it. "Will you come with me to a brunch in Phoenix next week?" the woman from my past asked. I didn't hesitate to answer, "Yes." When we arrived at the event later that week we found our seats at a round banquet table with eight other women. I estimated these ladies were all in their late seventies, maybe even eighty years old.

As my friend and I sat down, I noticed something uncanny about these women. They all looked alike. I don't mean because of their age, but rather their eyes, or their smiles, or something bore a look of familiarity. I wondered if maybe they were all somehow related. My friend noticed it too and whispered to me, "Aren't they beautiful?" They each glowed with an inner beauty, and I sensed a sweet spirit between them.

The older woman to my left chatted with us and asked about our background, and then we asked about her. "I came here with my friends," she said, gesturing to the ladies around the table. They all looked at her as she talked and nodded their heads knowingly. "We've all prayed together every week for the past several years," she explained.

That was it. The familiar look within their eyes reflected the Spirit of God at work in them, binding them closer than sisters, making them "one" in Jesus. I wanted to experience such unity in my life. After that brunch, my new-old friend and I met on several occasions to pray together, to help each other out in a pinch and to enjoy each other's company as our friendship blossomed. One afternoon she called and asked if I'd consider speaking at the women's retreat for her church.

"Will you be there?" I wanted to know. She assured me she would, and after talking about the details, I agreed to go. While Barak's response to Deborah's challenge may have grown out of fear, he unfortunately showed a lack of faith by refusing the job if Deborah didn't go with him. I prayed I would never go beyond fear into the arena of faithlessness, but I was happy to have a friend willing to "go with me" in this experience. And when Deborah joined her faith to Barak's fears and doubts, they agreed in spirit and acted together to honor God in a united effort. "If two of you on earth agree about anything you ask for, it will be done for you by my Father in heaven" (Matthew 18:19).

The following month at the retreat one of the ladies in the group commented to me how much I was like my friend. "You almost seem like sisters," she said. I laughed because I knew how completely opposite we were in personality. But my thoughts went back to the eight women at the brunch. I stopped and thanked God for his tender love in giving me the desire of my heart through the gift of friendship.

Actually, after praying for a best friend, God didn't answer me in the way I expected. Within a year after my daughters first asked, "Who's your best friend?" I realized God hadn't given me *one* best friend. He'd given me six! Today these same six women continue to encourage me to take risks, to be vulnerable and to persevere. Four of them came as a group package, and two as solo acts. They have so eased what I consider burdens and pressures that I wonder how I survived so long without them. They surround my life like a loom around a tapestry— sisters of the heart, shining with God's Spirit of unity.

Unceasing prayer unites you with other hearts devoted to God.

WEAVINGS

*Therefore, since we are surrounded by such a great cloud of witnesses,
let us throw off everything that hinders and the sin that so easily entangles,
and let us run with perseverance the race marked out for us. HEBREWS 12:1*

"The friends thou hast, and their adoption tried,
Grapple them to thy soul with hoops of steel."
William Shakespeare, *Hamlet,* act 1, scene 3

❊   ❊   ❊   ❊

Thank God for answering your prayers in friendships, even if he is still working it out in your life. Describe how friendships have enabled you to be the person God created you to be. Share these thoughts and blessings with the friends who have made such a difference.

Part 5

THE FIRST
STITCH

That first stitch, when the weaver's bobbin
passes from one side to the other,
reflects the moment when we move from
distant worship to a place of intimate love
inside the Holy of Holies.

✳   ✳   ✳   ✳

*And Ruth the Moabitess said to Naomi, "Let me go to the fields and pick up the
leftover grain behind anyone in whose eyes I find favor."... So she went out and
began to glean in the fields behind the harvesters. As it turned out, she found
herself working in a field belonging to Boaz.... Boaz asked the foreman of his
harvesters, "Whose young woman is that?"*

*The foreman replied, "She is a Moabitess who came back from Moab with
Naomi."...*

*So Boaz said to Ruth, ... "Watch the field where the men are harvesting, and
follow along after the girls. I have told the men not to touch you. And whenever you
are thirsty, go and get a drink from the water jars the men have filled."*

*At this, she bowed down with her face to the ground. She exclaimed, "Why have
I found such favor in your eyes that you notice me—a foreigner?"*

*Boaz replied, "I've been told all about what you have done for your mother-in-law
since the death of your husband.... May you be richly rewarded by the LORD, the
God of Israel, under whose wings you have come to take refuge."*

*"May I continue to find favor in your eyes, my LORD," she said. "You have given
me comfort and have spoken kindly to your servant."...*

At mealtime Boaz said to her, "Come over here. Have some bread and dip it in the wine vinegar."

When she sat down with the harvesters, he offered her some roasted grain. She ate all she wanted and had some left over. . . .

So Ruth stayed close to the servant girls of Boaz to glean until the barley and wheat harvests were finished. And she lived with her mother-in-law.

One day Naomi her mother-in-law said to her, "My daughter, should I not try to find a home for you, where you will be well provided for? Is not Boaz . . . a kinsman of ours? Tonight he will be winnowing barley on the threshing floor. . . . Go down to the threshing floor, but don't let him know you are there until he has finished eating and drinking. When he lies down, note the place where he is lying. Then go and uncover his feet and lie down. He will tell you what to do." . . .

When Boaz had finished eating and drinking and was in good spirits, he went over to lie down at the far end of the grain pile. Ruth approached quietly, uncovered his feet and lay down. In the middle of the night something startled the man, and he turned and discovered a woman lying at his feet.

"Who are you?" he asked.

"I am your servant Ruth," she said. "Spread the corner of your garment over me, since you are a kinsman-redeemer."

"The LORD bless you, my daughter," he replied. "This kindness is greater than that which you showed earlier: You have not run after the younger men, whether rich or poor. And now, my daughter, don't be afraid. I will do for you all you ask."

R U T H 2:2-3, 5-6, 8-14, 23; 3:1-11

13

Prepared

I breathed a sigh of relief when an entire day and night alone came as a gift from God. Early that morning I had kissed my husband goodby at the airport. Out-of-town business meant he wouldn't return until the following night. The kids were off on their own getaway with Grandma and Grandpa. So I was left all alone.

In the quiet I had trouble letting go of the chaotic picture of a typical day in my life. I remembered just a few mornings earlier digging through a pile of laundry looking for a semi-clean shirt to iron for my husband who was already late for work. The kids sat at the table eating bowls of Rice Krispies and fighting over who got the toy inside the box. I simply ignored the battle, tired of it all even before I'd eaten my breakfast. I'd been in this mode for several days. But now I was ready to be all alone, ready to cuddle up to the quiet.

I'd dreamed of a retreat like this, often saying, "I need time to myself, time to not be a mom or a wife or a coworker or church server. Time just to be me, alone with God." I wanted to read and pray and write more words in one sitting than I'd ever written before. For too many weeks and months I'd given of myself until my well ran dry. Fulfilling the needs of my own family required a tremendous amount of giving. Add to that my commitment to organize the children's ministry at church, and lead a local writer's group, and help in the classrooms at my children's school, all the while keeping up with routine chores at home, and I was one tired, burned-out woman.

I wonder if Ruth was on the edge of burnout when she came alone to the fields to glean grain behind the harvesters. Survival depended on Ruth's ability to find food for both herself and her mother-in-law, Naomi, since both their husbands had died. The fields of Boaz held possibility since he was a distant relative to Naomi's deceased husband. Living with a mother-in-law who, by her own admission, was bitter about life had to have its trying moments. Maybe that's why Ruth said to Naomi, "Let me go to the fields." Maybe she looked forward to time alone out in the fresh air, even if it meant hard physical labor.

My limited ability to give, out of my own energy, made my heart cry out to God, "Let me go to a place of solitude." I was determined to use this time as refreshment with God. I worshiped by reading the Psalms out loud to him, but felt odd doing it. I rarely read Scripture aloud unless called on in Sunday school. But in my quietness I found a freedom and power in speaking the Scriptures. Those words didn't float silently through my mind to mingle with my trivial thoughts and misguided ideas. These spoken words tumbled out like gold coins from a bag. They landed with a clink and lay there with shimmering truths—blessings to pick up from the field.

Ruth experienced the power of the spoken word when she met the man who, symbolically, represented her Lord and provider. When she spoke to Boaz there in the field, away from her normal demands of life, she bowed to the ground, giving him highest regard and honor, and thanking him for his kindness and favor. And when she bowed to him, he extended his hand of comfort and provided for her physically by offering her food and drink.

That's what this day meant to me. As I continued reading and worshiping, I sensed my Lord returning to the field where I had been picking up leftover blessings. But rather than allowing me to glean from the field, he extended his hand and said, "Come, eat at my table and drink from my cup." I was prepared to dine with my Master, and I knew this day would be an extraordinary, life-changing time of refreshment.

Unceasing prayer finds time alone with the Master.

WEAVINGS
As the deer pants for streams of water, so my soul pants for you, O God.
My soul thirsts for God, for the living God.
When can I go and meet with God? PSALM 42:1-2

"My God, what is a heart that thou shouldst it so eye, and woo,
Pouring upon it all thy art, as if thou hadst nothing else to do?"
George Herbert, quoted in *Clinging* by Emilie Griffin

❄   ❄   ❄   ❄

Consider the questions of Psalm 42. Take it literally, and ask yourself,
"When can I go and meet with God?" What place or time do you set
aside for meeting with him every day? Do you need a special day away
from your routine? Where can you find such a place?

14

The Other Side . . .

In my stillness I pondered how the past several months had sapped my
soul. How had I let myself get to this point of spiritual dryness? I
realized any regular time alone with God and in his Word had been
hit-or-miss. And when I did sit down with my Bible, I read with a
restless heart, skipping here and there, skimming through chapters or
entire books looking for . . . something. I think I was searching for words
of encouragement or inspiration or some other "motivator" to help me
continue giving. But I'd missed the most important step. I had failed to

look for *God*, and to hear the voice of the One speaking those words.

On this day alone, God called me to come to him, to come even beyond the veil of worship where he's on one side and I'm on the other. Although Christ's death ripped open that veil hiding the Holy of Holies, I'd rarely taken the time or found the courage to inch my way forward for a peek inside, let alone set foot into his presence. But now I was drawn to him. My Lord honored my thoughts toward him and graced my spirit with his peace and joy. His mercy was so great I never even had a chance to feel guilty about my failure to meet him in this way on a daily basis.

Ruth teaches me about the need to approach the Master in quietness and with a sense of patient expectancy. In the story of her life, she came back to Boaz at night. As he slept by the grain pile, she "approached him quietly and lay at his feet." Her tender approach and quieted heart spoke volumes of intimate love. And when Boaz sensed her there and asked what she wanted, she boldly answered, "Spread the corner of your garment over me, since you are my kinsman-redeemer."

Those words transport me to the foot of the cross where the soldiers took Jesus' garments and divided them among themselves, except for one seamless piece of cloth for which they cast lots (John 19:23-24). A seamless garment represented Jesus himself—whole and perfect. The corner of that garment, stained with holy blood, falls from the cross to cover my sin even though I'm as guilty as the soldiers who pulled the cloth from his body. Yet, because I call him my Savior, I see my sin and weakness. I know my need for the wholeness of a seamless garment, and I boldly request, "Spread the corner of your garment over me, since you are my kinsman-redeemer."

What shocks me more than anything about Ruth and Boaz is his response to her request. Even though she was a foreigner and he owed her nothing, he responded as God responds to me: "This kindness is greater than that which you showed earlier." Ruth's "earlier kindness" worshiped him. But her greater kindness loved him.

My desire for a more personal relationship with him, beyond my worship of him, showers God with kindness. My longing for personal involvement with him, beyond my wondering what I'll get in return, touches God with love. And for the first time I saw the vulnerability of God's heart. Just like me, he wants someone to show him kindness and faithfulness. How can I do anything but cry over a tenderhearted God and say, "Let it be me, Lord, let it be me."

Unceasing prayer blesses God with the kindness of a heart longing for him.

WEAVINGS
Thus I have become in his eyes like one bringing contentment.
Song of Songs 8:10

"How good of God to provide us a way into his heart."
Richard Foster, *Prayer: Finding the Heart's True Home*

❀   ❀   ❀   ❀   ❀

How could you describe the difference between being in love with God or being in awe of him? How do you view the possibility of a real love relationship with God? How can you create a time or place to approach him in quietness, in hushed expectancy, to explore the possibility of a deeper relationship?

15

. . . And Back Again

My time alone with God drew to an end the following evening. I hated to leave my retreat and the intimate love we had shared, but I knew it was time to get back to reality. I drove to the airport to pick up my husband and sensed God's continued nearness as he painted a brilliant sunset just for me. Awed and humbled, quiet before my God in these last minutes alone, I asked, "Is there one final lesson I must learn before taking calls for help from my family again?"

I heard no voices from heaven. Only this hushed realization prevailed: Alone for a time is refreshment, but it's not God's purpose for me right now. Even Adam, the only man to ever really be alone with God was incomplete in that state of being. And Eve wasn't put in the garden to get away from it all, but rather to come and help.

I had spent these hours alone with my Savior and eaten richly at his table. Now, like Ruth, I was full but still had food left on my plate. This, I knew was the key to giving. I had to continually come to the table to feast with the Lord of the Harvest. Ruth too went back to her reality of making a life for herself and her mother-in-law. Eventually she married Boaz and began building a family of her own, a family ultimately destined to bring the Messiah into the world.

Time with my Master, Creator and Friend refreshed my heart and encouraged me to find time each day to meet with him. Before the sun is up, I'm up to meet my Master alone. The only way I know to give without burning out is to come quietly and expectantly and lay my cares, my victories, my cries of mercy, at his feet every day.

Many have said, "How do you get up so early? I just don't have the time or energy to have quiet time every day." I think there's a point, like the tip of a needle, when taking time and making the effort pierces through the chore and emerges on the other side as joy. Just like Ruth working in the field to pick up what blessings she could, it was a chore at first. But she soon realized that behind her task of gleaning stood the joy of knowing Boaz, the lord of the field and her harvest. And when she understood that, she no longer saw it as a chore but rather a privilege. Then she came quietly and rested expectantly at his feet.

A few days after my retreat, I was back in my typical routines. I smiled as the girls ate their Rice Krispies and battled over the cereal toy. I ironed a clean white shirt for my husband because I wanted to do it, and I looked at it all with a new sense of thankfulness. And even as I worked and gave, I heard God speak his love in whispered tones that transcended the high pitch of a sibling squabble and the clatter of dishes and pans.

Unceasing prayer goes with God into the world with purpose.

WEAVINGS
In the morning, O Lord, you hear my voice; in the morning I lay my requests before you and wait in expectation. Psalm 5:3

"If we really mean to pray and want to pray, we must be ready to
do it now. These are only the first steps toward prayer,
but if we never make the first step with determination, we
will not reach the last one: The presence of God."
Mother Teresa, *Jesus, the Word to Be Spoken*

❋   ❋   ❋   ❋

How would you describe your time alone with God? Is it a chore or a joy? Write about an experience when you felt like you crossed that threshold from worship into knowing God in a more real, intimate way. Or tell him how you feel about the possibility—excited, frightened, unbelieving? He can handle your feelings.

Part 6
PATTERNS

The self-made patterns of life appear as gray,
uncertain shadows of thought. But with just a touch,
God defines the colors and patterns—
red blood, gold crowns, white robes—and stitches his
holiness into patterns of humanity.

❋   ❋   ❋   ❋

*A large crowd followed and pressed around [Jesus]. And a woman was there
who had been subject to bleeding for twelve years. She had suffered a great deal
under the care of many doctors and had spent all she had, yet instead of getting
better she grew worse. When she heard about Jesus, she came up behind him in
the crowd and touched his cloak, because she thought, "If I just touch his clothes,
I will be healed." Immediately her bleeding stopped and she felt in her body that
she was freed from her suffering.*

*At once Jesus realized that power had gone out from him. He turned around in
the crowd and asked, "Who touched my clothes?"*

*"You see the people crowding against you," his disciples answered, "and yet you
can ask, 'Who touched me?' "*

*But Jesus kept looking around to see who had done it. Then the woman, knowing
what had happened to her, came and fell at his feet and, trembling with fear, told him
the whole truth. He said to her, "Daughter, your faith has healed you. Go in peace
and be freed from your suffering."*

MARK 5:24-34

16

The Real Me

My girls were at school, my husband at work. I wandered the house, restless, bored and frustrated. Typical family problems hammered away at my peace. Where would we find the money to pay for the dental work we needed? How could we help our daughter with school problems? Small irritations, but enough to keep my mind in motion, unable to settle on any one task.

As usual, I ended up in the kitchen. Pouring a glass of milk, I reached for the cookie jar. Eight cookies and a final gulp later, I sat at the table, hating what I had just done. More than that, I hated how often I found myself in this overeating guilt trip pattern. I fought a constant battle with food and weight. Nearly forty pounds overweight, I found that food was winning. I wanted to lose the weight, but these unhealthy habits kept me chained, almost addicted, to the overeating process. I couldn't figure out why I deliberately did this to myself over and over, and I cried at the havoc wrought by my own twisted logic.

This was one area where unceasing prayer wasn't a problem. Continually I asked God for help. If I couldn't get rid of the behavior, couldn't he at least help me unwind the thoughts that led to errone-ous conclusions and harmful behavior? My mind and body weren't cooperating with each other. The more I ate, the further I sank into thinking I'd never be healthy. And the more unhealthy I felt, the less I wanted to do something about it.

The nameless woman who had been "bleeding for twelve years" must have battled a similar turmoil in her spirit. In that age, Judaic law labeled women "unclean" and "untouchable" even during a regular menstrual cycle. And if a physical condition caused the flow of blood to never stop, she became an outcast.

Add to that the teaching of the Pharisees that said physical ailments were God's punishment for sin, and you might have one disturbed woman—always hoping, always disappointed and always alone. If I listen to the silence of Scripture, I hear the story of this woman's life: no name, no family, no friends are mentioned. Her mind and body, no doubt, battled between the truth of who she really was and the person her body forced her to become—an outcast.

Like the bleeding woman, I looked to outside sources to help me deal with these symptoms of deeper problems. Scripture says the woman "suffered a great deal under the care of many physicians." She spent all her money, her time and her emotional strength to rid herself of her burden. I too had invested in weight-loss programs, diets and special foods, thinking if I could change the outer symptoms, the inner pain would disappear as well.

The sad truth was, like this woman, instead of getting better, I grew worse. An empty cookie jar stood as testament to my failure at fixing myself. All I knew was that "the real me" was hidden somewhere inside and I needed God's help to strip away these patterns of destruction.

Unceasing prayer lets God unveil the truth of who I am.

WEAVINGS
I do not understand what I do. For what I want to do I do not do,
but what I hate I do. . . . For I have the desire to do what is good, but I
cannot carry it out. ROMANS 7:15, 18

"Lord, do not stay thy hand, cut away until I am brought out into
the fair lines and lineaments of the image of God."
D.C. Hughes, quoted in *Becoming a Woman of Purpose*
by Cynthia Heald

❈   ❈   ❈   ❈

Are there areas of gray uncertainties in your life? Feelings that deceive you into acting in ways you really don't desire? Don't be afraid to look it in the eye. Take away the fuzzy gray by giving it form and substance through your journal.

17

The Root of
the Problem

"You've lost another half pound." The attendant reading the scale smiled as I weighed in for my weekly weight-loss meeting. "Oh joy," I thought, wishing it had been five. I wondered how long I would humiliate myself by letting someone else take charge of my weight loss rather than just simply eating healthy and exercising more. If history had anything to teach, my demise would occur when I failed to lose an ounce or two. Or, God forbid, when I *gained* a quarter pound.

I'd spent countless hours bemoaning my battle with weight, always on the lookout for someone or something to blame — everything from past rejections, to stress, to societal pressure put on women to look a certain way. Some days I cried like a victim, "Food controls me." Other days I pretended to be in charge and pretended not to care about my weight and proclaimed, "I'll eat what I want, when I want." Both arguments kept my tummy full, and my guilt complex fat.

I tried to "turn it all in God's direction," but I felt pushed and crowded by my own false attitudes and labels drawn from mixed messages, labels that say, "Thin is beautiful," but then again, "Eat, drink and be merry," but then again, "If you're going to eat, reduce the fat because . . . thin is beautiful." If I'm not thin does that mean I'm not beautiful? I wondered where Jesus was in the middle of this fray. I have to push so hard to reach him.

The bleeding woman broke through those confusing labels, broke through the pressing crowd, hoping no one saw who she was; she even broke the law to reach her healer. And when she did, a mere touch to the edge of his garment sent his healing power washing over her in sweet freedom from her suffering. Mark 5:9 is careful to specify she felt freed from her suffering *"in her body."* I wonder, if she had to choose, would she have chosen physical healing or emotional healing? Or, like me, did she find the two so twisted together into illogical patterns that they just couldn't be unraveled?

That touch was only the beginning of her story. Jesus knew she needed something beyond physical healing because he turned and asked one of those hard questions that cuts to the heart of the labels she'd placed on herself, the labels that defined and confined her. He asked, "Who *touched* me?" Why did he have to ask that? Why didn't he say, "Who was healed?" or "What just happened?"

Jesus knew her labels and lies needed to be torn away and the beauty of her personhood restored as much as her body needed healing. To the untouchable outcast, Jesus asked, "Who touched me?" She came forward and fell at his feet and told him the whole truth—how an unclean, imperfect woman came to touch his clean and perfect righteousness as her final hope for healing.

As I struggled one day, grieving over a death in the family, I caught myself in the arms of a false comforter. Food filled my emptiness at that moment, and, with the power of a sledgehammer, Christ's question came down hard. "Why do you need food?" I immediately responded almost in anger, "Because food won't leave me."

I wanted to grab my thoughts and swallow them up, but it was too late. I choked on my words as they revealed the idolatry of my false comfort. In that moment I knew I had soothed myself with temporary distractions of food and diets. It all sounds so acceptable and pleasing and right. But it's all so wrong when I use it to replace God's comfort.

I saw my sin strike another crucifying blow to my Savior. But even there on the cross his eyes begged me to reach for his sacrifice and feed on his compassion and understanding. I remembered his words, "I am the bread of life. Whoever comes to me will never be hungry, (John 6:35 NRSV)" so, "take, eat, this is my body which is broken for you" (2 Corinthians 11:24 KJV).

I no longer cared if I lost or gained another pound. I cared only that I not lose sight of my Savior in the crowd of false comforts, or in the loneliness of the cross. I, an imperfect woman, reached to touch the hem of perfect righteousness as my hope for healing, and I felt the labels and patterns begin to fall away.

Unceasing prayer breaks through labels,
which confine and define me, to reach out to Jesus.

WEAVINGS

For you created my inmost being; you knit me together in my mother's
womb. I praise you because I am fearfully and wonderfully made; your
works are wonderful, I know that full well. PSALM 139:14-15

"To walk in the light means that everything that is
of the darkness drives me closer into the centre of the light."
Oswald Chambers, *My Utmost for His Highest*

❖   ❖   ❖   ❖

What past pain or brokenness or physical challenge in your life do you identify with as you consider the story of the bleeding woman? Make a list of God's attributes or his promises, and place it next to your struggle. Ask God to stitch that list to your heart and make them reality.

18

Pushing Through

As I put these thoughts on paper, I continue the struggle of making Jesus Lord of the physical me. It hurts even to strike the keys that tap out this truth. I've fought for weeks with these words, trying to turn the gray haze hanging over this battlefield into crisp, black lines standing at attention on clean, white space.

It's hard because I'm disappointed over my continued wound, my thorn in the flesh that God seems to have chosen as his reminder of his grace in my weakness. And it's hard because I've pulled out the old "failure" label and restitched it to the seam of my soul, that place where my humanness bumps up against God's holiness and we wrestle to become one.

The bleeding woman's life was a give-and-take with Jesus that wrestled her humanness into submission through his holiness. After the body healing, after the hard questions and honest answers, Jesus spoke again. He reconfirmed her physical healing as a result of her faith. But he added to it the deep emotional healing with the words, "Go in peace and be freed from your suffering."

Be freed. That's different than saying she *was* freed. Jesus' word offers a continual, present tense, ongoing freedom from suffering. The word *suffer* in the original Greek context meant "to whip a criminal." This was the self-imposed, guilt-whipping suffering she would continue to carry with her if she didn't allow Jesus to address the entirety of her suffering. That's what guilt and suffering does to me. I label myself "criminal" for misusing food and "failure" for not conquering it. But I'm learning that those patterns and labels weren't stitched to my soul by my Creator. So I have to return to him over and over to experience that continual, present tense, ongoing healing.

I'm praying again today for Jesus to change my patterns of destruction. And one minute at a time, one choice at a time, I can decide to reach for the false comforts of this world, which only makes things worse. Or I can choose to build a life of prayer by continuing to push through the crowd of lies that try to keep me from reaching Jesus. So I'm pushing on to proclaim: "A number on the scale or a loss or a gain does not define who I am." I find myself when I willingly lose my sinful self to gain Christ and his healing touch.

To the woman with no name or family record, Jesus whispered a new name, "Daughter." To the outcast and law breaker part of who she was emotionally, he said, "Go in peace, be freed from your turmoil." When I think of the bleeding woman touching Jesus, that moment of healing symbolizes for me my bleeding heart flowing into his body and blood on the cross. And I see a new pattern for my life: His wounds for healing. His blood for me.

Unceasing prayer lets God heal body and spirit.

WEAVINGS
He himself bore our sins in his body on the tree,
so that we might die to sins and live for righteousness; by his
wounds you have been healed. 1 PETER 2:24

"I know thou hearest me because
A quiet peace comes down to me,
And fills the places where before
Weak thoughts were wandering wearily;
And deep within me it is calm,
Though waves are tossing outwardly."
Amy Carmichael, *Gold Cord*

❖   ❖   ❖   ❖

Read Isaiah 53, and revel in the richness of God's sacrifice on your behalf. Read Psalm 139, and revel in who you are in God's eyes.

Part 7

THE BOBBIN

The bobbin is the weaver's tool connecting fibers
together as one, just as worship becomes
the tool connecting my heart to God and God's heart
to mine until the two are one.

❁ ❁ ❁ ❁

*Now one of the Pharisees invited Jesus to have dinner with him, so he went to
the Pharisee's house and reclined at the table. When a woman who had lived a
sinful life in that town learned that Jesus was eating at the Pharisee's house,
she brought an alabaster jar of perfume, and as she stood behind him at his feet
weeping, she began to wet his feet with her tears. Then she wiped them with her
hair, kissed them and poured perfume on them.*

*When the Pharisee who had invited him saw this, he said to himself, "If this man
were a prophet, he would know who is touching him and what kind of woman she
is—that she is a sinner."*

*Then [Jesus] turned toward the woman and said to Simon, "Do you see this
woman? I came into your house. You did not give me any water for my feet, but she
wet my feet with her tears and wiped them with her hair. You did not give me a kiss,
but this woman, from the time I entered, has not stopped kissing my feet. You did
not put oil on my head, but she has poured perfume on my feet. Therefore, I tell you,
her many sins have been forgiven—for she loved much. But he who has been forgiven
little loves little."*

*Then Jesus said to her, "Your sins are forgiven. . . . Your faith has saved you; go
in peace."*

LUKE 7:36-50

19

A Prepared Heart

I remember the Sunday morning routines when my children were small. I coaxed my four-year-old into her shoes and socks, grabbed the baby's diaper bag and stuffed in diapers, bottles, wipes and toys. I strapped their squirming, little bodies into car seats, and sat in the car while my husband took his last-minute shower as we waited with utmost impatience. When he emerged, I mumbled with a martyr's sigh, "Finally, we're ready for worship!"

On one particular Sunday, I sat in the cushioned pew letting distracted thoughts guide me to the deep questions of life, like "Should we get hamburgers or tacos for lunch?" But after the benediction, the handshakes and smiles, I couldn't ignore a turbulance in my spirit. There was nothing wrong with the worship service in my church; it was my attitude that was lacking. My heart had drifted far from Jesus. I was uncomfortably full of myself and unknowingly starved for Christ's spirit.

Later that week God drew for me a vivid picture of true worship and unbounded love for Christ through the story of the weeping woman. That troubled spirit in me grew stronger as I considered the contrast between how I worshiped on Sunday compared to the depth of this woman's experience. When she came to Jesus, she wasn't waiting for church to begin so she could "get in the mood" to worship. In fact, she didn't get ready *for* worship, as though getting ready to watch a show. Nor did she sit back like Simon the Pharisee, an overstuffed pew potato full of spiritual insights but little action.

I can picture her entering Simon's house, and whispering to

someone at the door, "I want to see Jesus." Her worship was active, full of verbs—she brought, and stood weeping, she wet his feet, wiped them dry, kissed them and poured perfume. She came to Jesus heart-ready. She had prepared her heart to worship long before her arrival at Jesus' feet. She came boldly, and experienced richly the impact of his righteousness on her sinful life.

This is a dimension of worship I'm only beginning to experience in my life. I'm seldom heart-ready when the church bell rings. Even if we're on schedule, I haven't necessarily spent the preceding days humbling my heart and contemplating the gift I'll bring to Jesus. My worship seems to be turned inside out. Some weeks I realize the only trinity I've worshiped is me, myself and I. I arrive at church hoping to relinquish *my* burdens so *I* can experience freedom. *My* relief is the sole focus of any desire to bow before God. I rarely give him that awestruck gaze he so deserves.

But this weeping woman sought Jesus' face and fixed her entire purpose for living at that moment on him. She was able to put aside distractions, glares from on-lookers, the smell of a good meal. Nothing stopped her. Her actions didn't center on her needs or desires. She came to honor her Lord. And in doing so, Jesus gave her what she needed without her asking. Worshiping the Master precipitated her healing, her forgiveness, her restoration.

How can I enter a worship experience within my church, the body of Christ, when my only thoughts revolve around the inconveniences of getting there on time? I had a few lessons still to learn from the hands of a weeping woman.

Unceasing prayer worships the Creator, not the creation.

WEAVINGS
Ascribe to the Lord the glory due his name;
worship the Lord in the splendor of his holiness. Psalm 29:2

"As I enter into a relationship with Him, I find Him so compelling
that everyone and everything else pales in comparison to the
splendor of His presence. In beholding His glory, I am changed."
Jennifer Kennedy Dean, *Heart's Cry*

❀   ❀   ❀   ❀

What causes you or your family stress as you prepare for church on
Sunday morning? How can you plan ahead to alleviate those rough
spots? Identify your purpose for attending a church service, and lay that
thought before God. Ask him to search your heart and reveal new ways
for you to express your love for him.

20

Willing Hands

When I was a child, Sunday was the happiest day of my week. I don't
remember my parents being stressed out by it, nor do I remember
whining, "Do we have to go to church today?" Our everyday life
seemed to revolve around church. Mom was the pianist, so we sang
hymns and choruses all week while she practiced Sunday's music.
Anticipation mounted as we spent much of Saturday preparing for
the advent of Sunday. Mom took inventory for the after-church noon
meal. Dad helped us shine our shoes.

Next came the bath and shampoo ritual, ending with Mom
putting a head full of pin curls and plastic rollers first in my hair,
then my sister's. She wrapped a scarf around the curls with "bunny
ears" tied on top. We actually slept in those awful things all night
just to have that special hairdo on Sunday morning.

In the morning we were off to church bright and early. I brought my pennies for Sunday school offering, and believed the words to every chorus I sang: "Yes, Jesus loves me, the Bible tells me so." After Sunday school we joined Mom and Dad for the worship service (no junior church programs back then). Mom always kept two pretty hankies in her purse ready to make "babies in the cradle" to keep my sister and me occupied during the sermon.

On hot summer days, I often fell asleep during the service, my head resting on Daddy's knee. I was as comfortable there as if I'd been in my own bed. After the service, we said goodby with hugs and handshakes, and invited at least one family to share our noon meal.

We hurried home to pull the roast from the oven. Mom always worried it would be too dry. We gathered around the table as Dad blessed "the food and the hands that prepared it," then passed around pot roast cooked with potatoes and carrots, accompanied by fresh salad, buttered rolls, lemonade and chocolate cake for dessert. Conversing and laughing with friends at our table made home feel like church, or was church a part of my home? It all blended into one life for me.

Our hands were willing to worship and serve and join with others in love. We gave our best to honor God.

Those childhood memories seem closer to the heart of the weeping woman than my Sunday routines today. Her hands offered her best and ministered to Jesus in intimate ways—physical, tangible forms of worship expressing her heart-felt devotion. She poured expensive perfume to soothe his tired feet and wiped salty tears with her soft hair—natural symbols of her love and devotion to him.

Today, I fear I've built my church life into an awkward, protruding addition to our home. Sometimes I find myself at church out of habit or because of commitments. How I long for my worship to spring from a pure desire to meet Jesus. Instead I prod and plead to keep everyone on track and on time. My daughters go to their own Bible classes and child-geared worship. They're happy at church—maybe as happy as I was—but there's something, maybe a fading memory, that calls me to make Sunday the happiest day of the week. I miss the great anticipation as Sunday draws near. I miss the extended church family around our table at noon.

Maybe Jesus wants me to be a family builder within the church body, to create a place where families can come together as a continued act of worship and join hands around the table in my home. Instead of whining about cooking on Sunday, or complaining about the inconvenient time for worship service, maybe I can plan ahead and create that stability I once knew as a child. It's been a long time since I've made pot roast and potatoes. It's been a long time since home felt like church and church like home. It's been a long time since my heart and hands have offered their Sunday best to Jesus, or wept over the privilege of serving him in love.

Unceasing prayer lifts up hands willing to give to the body of Christ.

WEAVINGS
All the believers were together and had everything in common. . . .
They broke bread in their homes and ate together with glad and
sincere hearts. ACTS 2:44, 46

"The holiest moment of the church service is the moment when
God's people—strengthened by preaching and sacrament—
go out of the church door into the world to
be the Church. We don't go to church; we are the church."
Ernest Southcott, quoted in *The Body* by Charles Colson

❖   ❖   ❖   ❖

What can you do to include your church family in your activity during the week? Does Saturday evening and Sunday morning help or hinder your attitude toward worship? How can you blend your home life with your church life?

21

Holy Gifts

I laid my tithe in a silver offering plate, and watched with longing eyes as it passed hand to hand, making its way across the pew, down the aisle and out the sanctuary doors. "There go my new drapes," I shamelessly thought. More than once I've considered what God's money could have bought if left in my bank account. But with such an attitude, I think God may prefer a stop-payment on my check rather than a gift wrapped in resentment or tied up with regrets.

The woman weeping at Jesus' feet worshiped him by bringing her alabaster jar of costly perfume as a worship love offering—a symbol of her sinful life poured out at his feet. The very fragrance she used to entice other men into sin, she relinquished to Jesus. His acceptance made it holy. Material giving connects submission to service and heart to hands, in a lifestyle of worship that says, "All I have, beyond who I am, I give to you, Lord." This is worship that brings tangible, sacrificial gifts to Christ, pouring them out like perfume on his feet. Worshiping God with my material possessions becomes a sacred symbol of my total devotion to him.

What price do I pay to make my material offerings to God an act of worship, let alone sacrifice? True, my offerings will never buy God's grace, but when I give him my life, I'm agreeing to his lordship over my possessions as well. And when I worship with my heart ready, and my hands willing to serve, then my material gifts become a holy gift of love.

I still battle the stressed-out Sunday-morning routines on occasion, but I've made a new commitment to prepare for worship all week long. I search for ways to integrate it into my lifestyle and my daily habits.

I worship Jesus when I hike a mountain with my family, or share a meal with another family or pray with my children at bedtime.

Just this morning after dropping the kids off at school, I was awestruck by God's presence. Right in the middle of traffic, with a coffee cup in my hand, I wept over the incredible realization that I am his child and he's my Father.

Such moments of worship don't happen every day, but I'm beginning to praise him even for the lessons in patience as I wait in the car for my husband to finish his last-minute shower. Now when he emerges, I can say with sincerity, "I'm ready *to* worship," because I've prepared my heart, used my hands and offered him the gift of my life all week long.

True worship grows out of an ever-deepening relationship with God—a relationship which delights in him all week long, enabling me to come heart-ready to worship, expecting to see Jesus. This new spirit of worship connects my heart to God and God's heart to mine, like a weaver's bobbin connecting fibers of thread as one. But above all, I'm finding I can't truly worship without first breathing that plea, whispered from a weeping woman's heart, "I want to see Jesus."

Unceasing prayer offers heart, hands and holy gifts as an act of worship.

WEAVINGS
Therefore, I urge you . . . in view of God's mercy, to offer your bodies as living sacrifices, holy and pleasing to God—this is your spiritual act of worship. Romans 12:1

"God, I pray Thee, light these idle sticks of my life and may I burn for Thee. Consume my life, my God, for it is Thine."
Jim Elliot, quoted in *Shadow of the Almighty* by Elisabeth Elliot

❊   ❊   ❊   ❊

Romans 12:1 refers to the physical offering of yourself to God as an act of worship. Take a physical inventory of all you possess and ask God to help you discern what he wants you to have. Offer the rest to him.

Part 8

THE ART

Stitches of spiritual growth and personal progress reveal
the beauty of art in the tapestry of life.
But when I push with my own passion and pull with
self-made success, God stops all the
motion and says, "The beauty is not in the weaving,
but in the Weaver."

❈   ❈   ❈   ❈

*As Jesus and his disciples were on their way, he came to a village where a woman
named Martha opened her home to him. She had a sister called Mary, who sat
at the Lord's feet listening to what he said. But Martha was distracted by all
the preparations that had to be made. She came to him and asked, "Lord, don't
you care that my sister has left me to do the work by myself? Tell her to help
me!"*

*"Martha, Martha," the Lord answered, "you are worried and upset about many
things, but only one thing is needed. Mary has chosen what is better, and it will not
be taken away from her."*

LUKE 10:38-42

22

My Passion

At a recent writers conference a woman behind me in the lunch buffet line asked, "So what's your passion?"

Unsure where this conversation was headed, I looked toward the dessert table. My eyes lit up at the sight of my favorite—chocolate brownies. "Oh, my passion." I nodded knowingly. "Chocolate," I replied, half in jest.

"Chocolate." She squinted her eyes in serious contemplation. "That's interesting. How do you use it in your ministry?"

"Wait a minute," I said, chuckling, "I'm not sure we're on the same channel here. What's *your* passion?"

She didn't hesitate. "Single moms. I'm one myself, and God's laid it on my heart to help single moms."

Now I remembered. Several times our instructors had reiterated, "Write out of your passion . . . what you feel deeply about . . . what really excites you."

"I'm not sure what my passion is," I admitted. "But right now I'm passionate about writing in general."

Martha had a passion. And she used it in ministry. She opened her home on more than one occasion to Jesus and his followers. She loved to make things comfortable, delectable, inviting to her visitors. By any Christian standard, Martha had a gift of hospitality, and she was putting it to good use by serving others.

That's how I felt about writing. I wanted to write more than anything and even felt gifted in this area of communication. I took great joy in forming and reforming words and sentences, building paragraph upon paragraph, like a sculptor forming and reforming the clay. I ran every thread of information, every interaction, every thought and feeling, even every Scripture and prayer through the writing mill in my mind. And it seemed to pay off. God held open the doors of opportunity as I found early success in my attempts at writing, publishing several articles in well-known Christian publications. The thrill of that success kept me going, always looking for a new notch in my publishing belt. Certainly this was how God wanted me to use my time.

But without warning, the stitches of success in my tapestry began to unravel. For over a year no one wanted my work. Maybe it was a fluke I had come this far. The more I wrote and sought publication, (I called it being a good steward of the gift) the more distant I felt from God. Now he seemed to be closing all the doors in my face. Rejection after rejection lined my mailbox. Unfortunately, I didn't take this as a message from God. I am not a writer easily turned back by rejection. It spurred me on to keep trying.

But eventually, like Martha, I began to sense something wasn't right. My prayer turned from joy to complaint. "It just doesn't seem fair, Lord. I try to honor you with my success. Don't you want me to use this gift you've given? Don't you want me to use my writing to spread your word?" I don't know what I was thinking. Was I trying to make God feel guilty so he'd change his mind? I sounded desperate even to myself, and my questions sounded a bit like Martha's, "Don't you care, Lord?" I was ready to do whatever he asked. With pen poised, I listened for his voice.

Unceasing prayer lets God pull passion and purpose together as one.

WEAVINGS
Never be lacking in zeal, but keep your spiritual fervor, serving the Lord.
Romans 12:11

"Remember your avowed purpose, and keep ever
before you the likeness of Christ crucified."
Thomas à Kempis, *The Imitation of Christ*

❈   ❈   ❈   ❈

Do you have a passion that excites you? Something you feel compelled
to do or try or change? Turn to God with this passion, and ask him to
open your eyes to his perspective on it.

23

Progress Stopped

Just to be sure, I decided to spend some time studying and praying over
my writing career. I looked for the passions of men and women in the
Bible. But that word seemed to be absent from Scripture except when
referring to sin and once in the King James Version referring to Christ's
pain and suffering. I didn't like where this was heading.

What about the ministry of some of the people in the Bible? Again,
I didn't find many folks anxious for the jobs chosen for them by God.
Sure, most obeyed and gladly responded out of their love for God.
But Moses wasn't passionate about his assignment, nor was Jonah.
I don't think Paul was begging God to let him join the Christians
when his assignment changed. Some used their natural abilities to
serve God. Barnabas, for instance, who naturally encouraged others,
didn't get to sit around and write books about it. He had to live it,
not write it. I saw for the first time that all these people found their
happiness not in the job, but in serving their Creator and joining him
in his work.

If I serve God only when I'm passionate about something, then I may miss being used by him in areas that challenge me, stretch me, even frustrate me. Maybe I was using my passion for writing as a safety shield, to make me look good. That way I'd never be embarrassed by my inability or immaturity in another area of ministry.

The hard questions began to form in my mind: If I take away my passion for writing, where do I stand in my faith? Without my writing, what kind of relationship do I have with Jesus? Take away my passion and what or whom do I serve? I had to admit, without my writing I felt lost, alone and dissatisfied with life. How could I have let this get so out of hand—so out of God's hands? Writing consumed me. Honestly, my own need and desire for success and the praise of others had consumed me.

When Martha ministered in her home, her passion distracted her from her true purpose and source of happiness. I think she believed, as I did, that her serving deserved God's blessings, that she somehow had earned his favor for this effort. That attitude naturally turned to resentment. That's when Jesus called her to sit this one out for a while. To let go of the doing and come sit in his giving.

It was time for me to let go of the writing, to sit this one out for a while. I gave it all back to God to hold until he was ready, if ever, to let me write again. I thought I would feel resentful, but in that moment when God stopped the writing, all I felt was deeply loved by him. I'd been so busy pushing and pulling the stitches with my own passion and power that I hadn't realized how much I'd missed the relationship. So I laid down my pen and determined to pick it up only when, or if, he told me to. I let go of all my writing, journaling, writer's groups, conferences, even subscriptions to writer's magazines. As I did, God stripped away all the passions that encumbered me on my walk with him.

At first I felt lost. I'd actually forgotten how to pray without writing my prayers in a journal. But slowly, God drew me back into intimate fellowship with him, and I began to worship him again. My satisfaction and purpose in life lie not in my gifts, but in my relationship with the Giver of the gifts. When I was praying, "Don't you want me to succeed? Don't you want me to—" He stopped me and answered, "I just want you, period."

Unceasing prayer releases all that encumbers me,
even my passions, so I can enjoy my relationship with God.

WEAVINGS
They exchanged the truth of God for a lie,
and worshiped and served created things rather than the Creator—
who is forever praised. Amen. ROMANS 1:25

"We need not fear that in seeking God only we may narrow our lives or restrict the motions of our expanding hearts.
The opposite is true. We can well afford to make God All, to concentrate, to sacrifice the many for the One."
A. W. Tozer, *The Pursuit of God*

❊   ❊   ❊   ❊

If you took away your ability to do what you enjoy doing, even within the context of ministry, where would that leave you in your relationship to Christ? Is he still above all?

24

A Stitch at a Time

Nearly a year after I'd laid down my pen, I unwrapped a gift from my mom. I tried not to act like an excited little girl on her birthday. The package felt like a book. We both shared a love for good books and never tired of giving or receiving the perfect read. I ripped the paper and let it fall to the floor. Indeed, the gift was a book, but inside all the pages were blank—a journal. I looked at it and rubbed my hand over the floral cloth cover. I felt again like a child, but this time one holding forbidden matches. "Thanks, Mom," I said quietly.

She sensed my reluctance and said, "You need to start writing." Mom is a woman of God, and I wondered if this was his message too, his "All clear, you're good to go." I took the journal home and prayed, "Lord, do you want me to write in this?" I didn't hear any direct answer, only a peace, a release from my "time out." So I picked up a pen, and I began to write again.

This time, however, I felt hesitant. I never wanted to trade my relationship with my Father for the pleasure of writing. So I wrote for a period of time only to God. He alone was my reader and editor. I tested my thoughts and ideas before the One who put them there. I sought his counsel in how to be used again. Eventually he allowed me to share my words with others. The doors pushed open.

I returned to Martha's story, looking for her words, her prayer, her response to Jesus' call to come sit at his feet. But the story ended with Jesus' words, not Martha's. I don't know how he changed her life. I don't know if she obeyed. But I do know the next time Martha appears in Scripture, she's left her house guests inside while she runs to meet Jesus—not something the old Martha would have done (John 11:19-20). I think she'd learned her lesson.

I'd learned one too. God led me to this single conclusion: I exist for only one purpose—to love God with all the passion I possess. It's recorded over and over again, "Only *one* thing is needed," Jesus said to a busy and distracted Martha. And the Israelites were commanded, "Fear the LORD your God, serve him *only*" (Deuteronomy 6:13).

All my service and ministry and love for others isn't the root of my passion. It's only the passion fruit springing from a passion rooted in being loved by God and loving him in return. All he asks of me is to abide and remain in him. He is the vine; I am the branch. Whether I'm writing or resting, serving or praying, I'll never stop sitting at his feet for God alone is my passion.

Unceasing prayer is rooted in a passion for God alone.

WEAVINGS
But whatever was to my profit I now consider loss for the sake of Christ.
What is more, I consider everything a loss compared to the
surpassing greatness of knowing Christ Jesus my LORD, for whose sake I
have lost all things. I consider them rubbish, that I may gain
Christ and be found in him, not having a righteousness of my own . . .
but that which is through faith in Christ—the righteousness
that comes from God and is by faith. PHILIPPIANS 3:7-9

"If, without any side glances, we have only God in view, it is He,
indeed, who does what we do."
Meister Eckhart, quoted in *Markings* by Dag Hammarskjöld

❈   ❈   ❈   ❈

Make a list of all the things in your life you feel are the most precious.

They can be people, jobs, future plans, hopes, possessions. Be honest with yourself in preparing your list. Now turn each of those items in God's direction, and ask him to give you a pure heart toward them all. Ask him to remove any idolatrous thoughts toward them. Ask him to become the Lord over all.

Part 9

LOOSE ENDS

Even as God creates beauty in the tapestry of life,
negative thoughts hang like loose ends on
the back side of the tapestry. But one by one,
he ties them up, anchoring us in spirit and in truth
with his persistent love.

❖   ❖   ❖   ❖

*So [Jesus] came to a town in Samaria. . . . Jacob's well was there, and Jesus,
tired as he was from the journey, sat down by the well. It was about the sixth
hour.*

*When a Samaritan woman came to draw water, Jesus said to her, "Will you give
me a drink?" (His disciples had gone into the town to buy food.)*

*The Samaritan woman said to him, "You are a Jew and I am a Samaritan
woman. How can you ask me for a drink?" (For Jews do not associate with
Samaritans.)*

*Jesus answered her, "If you knew the gift of God and who it is that asks you for
a drink, you would have asked him and he would have given you living water."*

*"Sir," the woman said, "you have nothing to draw with and the well is deep. Where
can you get this living water? Are you greater than our father Jacob, who gave us
the well and drank from it himself, as did also his sons and his flocks and herds?"*

*Jesus answered, "Everyone who drinks this water will be thirsty again, but
whoever drinks the water I give him will never thirst. Indeed, the water I give him
will become in him a spring of water welling up to eternal life."*

*The woman said to him, "Sir, give me this water so that I won't get thirsty and
have to keep coming here to draw water."*

He told her, "Go, call your husband and come back."

"I have no husband," she replied.

Jesus said to her, "You are right when you say you have no husband. The fact is, you have had five husbands, and the man you now have is not your husband. What you have just said is quite true."

"Sir," the woman said, "I can see that you are a prophet. Our fathers worshiped on this mountain, but you Jews claim that the place where we must worship is in Jerusalem."

Jesus declared, "Believe me, woman, a time is coming when you will worship the Father neither on this mountain nor in Jerusalem. You Samaritans worship what you do not know; we worship what we do know, for salvation is from the Jews. Yet a time is coming and has now come when the true worshipers will worship the Father in spirit and truth, for they are the kind of worshipers the Father seeks. God is spirit, and his worshipers must worship in spirit and in truth."

The woman said, "I know that Messiah" (called Christ) "is coming. When he comes, he will explain everything to us."

Then Jesus declared, "I who speak to you am he."

J O H N   4 : 5 - 2 6

25

Hanging by a Thread

"Are we out of bread again?" my husband mumbled in frustration as he shoved the ham and mayo back into the fridge.

It was a simple question that could have been answered with a "yes" or "no." Instead, I countered defensively, "Why don't you ever notice anything I do right?"

"I'm not blaming you," he tried to assure me.

"Well you're not taking responsibility for the problem either. You have no idea what it's like being home all day with two little kids," I whined, unwilling to let it go.

I'd fired the first shot. Now he loaded his weapon. "And you have no idea what it's like to work in a pressure-cooker job and then come home to more stress. I just want a ham sandwich. I'd even make it myself . . . *if* we had any bread!"

This was the same argument we had had over and over again for more months than I care to admit. It wasn't always about ham sandwiches. Sometimes it was something really big, like why he didn't take out the garbage, or how I had no system for doing the laundry or why he never finished a project.

I felt stuck in an episode of "Seinfeld"—arguing about nothing meaningful for too many seasons. No one ever won, and we were both tired of the constant battles. The marriage knot we tied six years earlier now dangled like two loose ends, leaving our relationship hanging by a thin thread. We had raised our defensive shields as we blamed the other for not living up to expectations about everything from bread to sex.

At Jacob's well, Jesus also asked a simple question, easily answered with a "yes" or "no." He said, "Will you give me a drink?" But the woman at the well, just like me, put on her fighting gloves and put up her defenses. She hurled excuse after excuse, never really answering his question. She defined herself and those around her based on her inabilities rather than her abilities. Her excuses covered everything from family heritage, to a trivial discussion over drawing water from a well with no pitcher. And, I couldn't ignore their conversation about her marital status. Her heart prayer rang in low tones of "I'm not . . . I can't . . . you aren't . . . you can't."

Maybe that was my problem. Although I never asked him, I'm sure my husband would have agreed that our wedding bells now rang out those same low tones of defeat. We had come to define ourselves and each other by our inabilities rather than our abilities. When we fail to acknowledge who we are as gifts from God, then it's hard to honestly accept the reality of who we aren't.

When I communicate in habitually negative overtones of "I'm not . . . I can't . . . you aren't . . . you can't," then I become tone deaf, like the woman at the well, unable to hear and receive the message of encouragement and hope chiming deep within. And if such an attitude permeated my earthly relationships, how was it affecting my relationship with Christ?

Unceasing prayer brings all I am, and all I'm not, to Jesus.

WEAVINGS
[Love] is not rude, it is not self-seeking, it is not easily angered, it keeps no record of wrongs. 1 CORINTHIANS 13:5

"We are wounded by broken relationships, by the inexplicable iron curtains that hang in heart and soul between people. . . . Yet God is wounded when his children war; . . . God hurts when his

children don't love the way he intended for us to love."
Karen Burton Mains, *With My Whole Heart*

❀   ❀   ❀   ❀

Take inventory of your present attitudes toward others. Do your conversations sound defeated or hopeless? Turn your attitudes, positive or negative, toward God, and let his light open your eyes.

26

Threadbare Facts

I can't pinpoint exactly how or when or why we began this systematic shutdown of our relationship. We both had our complaints: I saw my husband as a workaholic. He seemed to care more about his job and coworkers than he did about his family—and me in particular. But then, he saw me as a nag. I criticized him when he worked long days or "wasted" an hour once a month socializing with coworkers. I often wondered why he chose to spend more time in the stress and hassle of the workplace when he could experience it in the comfort of his own home.

After six years of marriage we felt unconnected from each other. The thread that had woven our hearts together looked frayed, worn bare from the constant pull of bickering over unmet expectations. Even though the arguments sounded trivial—okay, childish—we did agree on one thing: That thread holding us together wasn't love or a romantic feeling. That thread was a promise, a vow made to God and each other to never cut the connection. We didn't *feel* it, but we *knew* it as a fact. And on that threadbare fact we hung our hope to rebuild a positive lifestyle together.

That woman at the well knew all about unmet expectations. The Jews rejected her as a Samaritan—not good enough to be a full-blooded Jew. Her community rejected her as a misfit—not good enough to draw water with the other women in the cool morning hours. And man after man rejected her—not good enough to be a wife.

But when Jesus talked with her, he took all those frayed rejections, dangling like loose ends, and began tying them, one excuse and one hurt at a time, with his persistent love. Jesus knew she possessed something no one could destroy—her spirit and the truth. No one could break her spirit or cut that shred of truth on which she hung all her hopes. "I *know*," she said, "I *know* that the Messiah will come." That fact, not a feeling, couldn't be denied. There she found the courage to hang on.

Trusting that truth, she took a vulnerable step. She placed her final hope of a Messiah in Jesus' hands. And he didn't disappoint her. He held out a cup of living water, and she drank in the satisfaction of a promise kept, an expectation met. In essence he said, "I'll meet your final expectation, your final thread of hope. I'll not disappoint you. I am your Messiah. I who speak to you am he."

After meeting Jesus, the woman at the well laid down her pitcher, the symbol of her rejection by the Jews and her community. She willingly returned to those people who had rejected her and had crushed her expectations. She was willing to try again, this time taking the unbreakable promise of Jesus with her.

Could living water save my dying marriage? Could he nurture new life in this home and this heart? Basing a marriage on a mere fact, a single promise, sounded so . . . so unromantic. Was this just one more broken expectation? My husband and I were willing to find out. We laid down the sin of our bad attitudes. We put aside our disappointments and decided to go to work on our marriage.

Unceasing prayer lets truth speak when feelings fail.

WEAVINGS
Show me your ways, O L<small>ORD</small>, teach me your paths; guide me in your truth and teach me, for you are God my Savior, and my hope is in you all day long. P<small>SALM</small> 25:4-5

"The prayer of the heart is a prayer that does not allow us to limit
our relationship with God to interesting words or
pious emotions. By its very nature such prayer transforms our
whole being into Christ precisely because it opens
the eyes of our soul to the truth of ourselves as well
as the truth of God."
Henri J. M. Nouwen, *The Way of the Heart*

❀   ❀   ❀   ❀

Who are the difficult people to love in your life? How have your feelings, positive or negative, affected your ability to love them? Ask Christ what step you can take next as he teaches you how to love. Be assured that he walks with you each step of the way.

27

Tying the Knot

I picked up the phone and dialed the number given to me by a friend. "So it's come down to this?" I thought as I waited for someone to answer the phone at the offices of a recommended marriage counselor. I ranked counseling right up there with letting someone go through my dirty laundry—humiliating at best. But within forty-eight hours my husband and I were sitting on a beige-and-brown plaid couch, chit-chatting with the counselor. I noticed boxes of tissues strategically placed nearby and wondered if I'd need them.

After spending months arguing over every triviality of life, it sounded ridiculous trying to express our complaints to a stranger, so we didn't. We generalized our problems, answered a few questions, and sat there looking at the counselor, wondering what to say next. He gave a reassuring smile and then these simple instructions: "This week I want you to think about what first attracted you to each other. What qualities did you value? Then bring back your lists next week."

I wondered if he too needed a list to help him understand why we had ever married each other, or perhaps he had another plan. The next week we returned with smiles on our faces. As the best counselors always do, he let us discover the plan on our own. Thinking about the other's positive qualities gave us time to look at the bright side of our marriage, to come out of the darkness. We reconsidered the truth of who we are in Christ, and for the first time in months, I felt positive and hopeful about our future. A simple direction turned us back to each other, tying strong knots of truth in place of our loose ends of half-truth.

Jesus gave the woman at the well a simple instruction. "Go, call your husband and come back." And here she had to reconsider the truth. "I have no husband," she said in half-truth. But Jesus didn't want her to worship in spirit and *half*-truth. He reminded her that the man she was living with wasn't her husband. After that, things changed. She was able to embrace the whole truth about herself and about Jesus. It enabled her to return to the town that had rejected her. She spoke to her neighbors, maybe for the first time in a long time, and persuaded them to come meet Jesus (vv. 28-30). Eventually, they spoke to her as well, almost thanking her for bringing them to Jesus (v. 42).

Meeting Jesus didn't instantly change everyone into loving neighbors. Jesus and his disciples stayed in their town several days,

(vv. 39-42). It required a process of learning and changing and growing. But Jesus' persistent love prevailed not only in bringing many people to the Father, but in turning a negative woman into a positive woman. His love didn't allow her negative defenses to turn him away. He tied the loose ends of her disappointments to his heartstrings.

He did the same for my husband and me. The simple instruction and truth spoken through the counselor didn't lead us down an instant path of happiness and smiles. It requires an ongoing process of learning and changing and growing. In our case, it gave us an anchor of truth to hold us steady as we uncovered deeper problems — issues of loneliness even within our marriage, addictive behaviors, desires and dependencies on the world rather than on God. But Christ's persistent love keeps us turned toward him. We're tied to each other, and together the three of us become one.

Unceasing prayer is anchored by Christ's persistent love.

WEAVINGS
I led them with cords of human kindness, with ties of love. HOSEA 11:4

"God's love to me is inexhaustible, and I must love others
from the bedrock of God's love to me."
Oswald Chambers, *My Utmost for His Highest*

❖   ❖   ❖   ❖

Read 1 Corinthians 13. As you look at your relationships, consider what difference Jesus has made or can make. Tie him into your conversation, your attitudes, your expectations. How would he act? What would he say? His love will make the difference.

Part 10
COLOR

Heritage and family, tradition and home,
rooting and uprooting, coming and going. Only when we
step back and look where we have been
do we see the rich color woven deep in a heart
on pilgrimage with God.

❊   ❊   ❊   ❊

Then the disciples went back to their homes, but Mary [Magdelene] stood
outside the tomb crying. As she wept, she bent over to look into the tomb and saw
two angels in white, seated where Jesus' body had been, one at the head and the
other at the foot.

They asked her, "Woman, why are you crying?"

"They have taken my Lord away," she said, "and I don't know where they have
put him." At this, she turned around and saw Jesus standing there, but she did not
realize that it was Jesus.

"Woman," he said, "why are you crying? Who is it you are looking for?"

Thinking he was the gardener, she said, "Sir, if you have carried him away, tell
me where you have put him, and I will get him."

Jesus said to her, "Mary."

She turned toward him and cried out in Aramaic, "Rabboni!" (which means Teacher).

Jesus said, "Do not hold on to me, for I have not yet returned to the Father. Go
instead to my brothers and tell them, 'I am returning to my Father and your Father,
to my God and your God.' "

Mary Magdalene went to the disciples with the news: "I have seen the Lord!" And
she told them that he had said these things to her.

J O H N   2 0 : 1 0 - 1 8

28

Roots

I looked out the picture window of the big farmhouse in the heartland of Indiana. Holding a cup of steaming coffee, I surveyed the mid-February coldness that had painted the land gray and brown. It looked weary and wounded, covered with snow and ice bandages. But frozen into that land were summer-soft memories of my childhood.

In 1905 my great-grandfather built this home where my grandpa, my mom, her brothers and some of my cousins were all born and raised. Although I have never lived there, I always feel like I'm coming home when I visit. I spent many summer days in the late fifties and early sixties husking corn, snapping green beans and drinking cold sugar tea on the porch swing. I climbed stacks of hay in the barn, played in the sprinklers or rode the tractor with Grandpa or an uncle down the gravel road.

On hot sticky evenings we all gathered under the giant box elder tree near the back porch hoping to catch a light breeze as we chased fireflies. We waited for the women to emerge from the house with a wooden bucket, a bag of rock salt and a tin cylinder full of sweet vanilla cream for the men to crank into ice cream. Life in this clan was worth savoring—sweet laughter, good natured wrestling and challenges, hearty hugs whenever any child wandered within an arm's reach of an adult. As I basked in the warmth of a loving family, my roots in life grew deep and wide, like the ancient roots beneath my bare feet.

An idyllic childhood and a loving family make clinging to earthly roots easy. But as I grew, those same roots made clinging to God feel unnecessary until I arrived at a day like today. With Grandpa's funeral just hours away, this was a day when I could no longer ignore the fact that these human lives and traditions would pass and leave me without a lasting anchor. Even a near-perfect childhood can lead to emptiness and a longing for satisfaction that God alone can fill.

Mary Magdalene's story reveals this same process of spiritual growth all within one single event in her life, within a single moment of prayer. At the empty tomb she encountered two angels who spoke to her. But even heavenly messengers were no substitute for Jesus. I've thought, "If I only saw an angel, or someone would confirm that what God says is true, then I could believe." I've heard others say, "If I only had a good childhood or a loving family, then I could believe." I have to stop putting angels or other people or my heritage or anything else in the place of Jesus. They only get in the way of meeting him face to face on my own. Only Jesus can satisfy a soul created to worship him.

My family and my heritage may point me in the right direction to find Jesus, as the angels did for Mary, but they can't replace him as the satisfaction of my life. My prayer that cold morning was "There has to be more. I'm looking for Jesus. Where have you taken him?"

Unceasing prayer casts aside all obstacles, even comforts, to find Jesus.

WEAVINGS
Anyone who loves his father or mother more than
me is not worthy of me; anyone who loves his son or daughter
more than me is not worthy of me. Matthew 10:37

"The autumn winds of a fading generation have blown me to this
cold rocky shore, and I want to know what life is here.
Can it be so cold as to snuff the fire out, so dark as to
extinguish the flame?"
John Fischer, *Making Real What I Already Believe*

❖   ❖   ❖   ❖

Looking back on your past, what events or people helped shape your life and your faith? Do these things control how you serve the Lord, or have you turned them over to him to use for his purposes?

29

Uprooting

Like generation upon generation, I grew and matured in this close-knit clan until it was time to uproot where I'd grown up and stand on my own. And while I longed for that day, the reality of it all felt more like being torn from the ground with my roots dangling like raw nerves, reaching for solid ground and nourishment.

Unfortunately, I set some of my roots into rocky soil, a difficult place to grow. Some of my poor choices in life touched those dangling nerves now and again—obstacles in relationships, changes and adjustments, and hard lessons to learn. I knew I needed to remain planted in Christ. I needed more than my Christian lifestyle. It was time to decide on my own, "Is this relationship with Jesus real, and is it for me?"

Mary must have questioned too in that garden as she looked for Jesus. Scripture says the disciples returned to their homes, leaving her standing all alone, on her own. Would she continue to search? Would she believe all by herself, or would she need that circle of friends, family or traditions to bolster her faith? Would she follow a lifestyle or follow Jesus?

With all her earthly supports gone, Jesus came to her and called her by name. "Mary." That personal recognition made all the difference in the world. She was his sheep, and a sheep listens for the shepherd's voice and recognizes it. When he spoke her name, she knew him and worshiped him. She wanted to touch him, and her response is recorded with an exclamation point. "Teacher!" What a relief to find Jesus. Now she knew for herself that this relationship was real, and it was hers, not some contrived religious rhetoric.

Coming full circle, I returned to words from my childhood that echoed in my mind. But this time it wasn't a little song I learned and memorized. These words sang from my heart, confirming with an exclamation point this truth, "Yes, Jesus loves me!" I sang it back to him as a love song. This was my relationship with Jesus, not something contrived.

My relief in finding Jesus came in small doses of gentle reality in the days, months and years to follow. His comfort, his peace, his forgiveness have renewed my heart and mind again and again. He restitched where my roots had torn and my nerves hung raw. We walked alone, other supports stripped away. I worshiped him, and was nourished by pure love directly from my Master's hand.

Unceasing prayer clings to Jesus for spiritual nourishment and growth.

WEAVINGS
My soul clings to you; your right hand upholds me. PSALM 63:8

"There is only one relationship that matters and that is
your personal relationship to the personal Redeemer and Lord.
Let everything else go, but maintain that at all costs,
and God will fulfill His purpose through your life."
Oswald Chambers, *My Utmost for His Highest*

❖   ❖   ❖   ❖

What steps have you taken to develop your own relationship with Christ? How does it differ from your parent's or grandparent's? How is it the same?

30

Branches

I dreaded this day but knew it would inevitably come. I had arrived in Indiana along with aunts, uncles, cousins, and friends to say goodby to Grandpa who had passed away a few days earlier at the age of eighty-eight. Several of us stayed with my aunt and uncle in the family farmhouse where they lived, but still it felt empty without Grandpa. This dread grew from my fear, held over many years, that with the passing of my family, I'd find my world a bit darker, matching the cold painting outside. I feared life would never be the same.

Was that Mary's first thought when Jesus said, "Don't touch me?" He'd always held out helping hands and hugs before. Now it seemed life would be different. But those weren't Jesus' final words to her. He wanted her to grow past the need to be held and hand fed forever. He was preparing her to go out and serve him in new ways, to start spreading the good news that he had risen.

Now was the time for me to begin to see a new direction as well. Something wonderful happened inside me while I was there at the farm surrounded by family. I saw my roots were not dying with Grandpa's death. They weren't even being uprooted. It was simply time to grow up a little, to stop worrying about being fed and pampered and to let Jesus begin producing fruit in my life to feed others.

I used to believe all these people, my kinfolk, were the source of my security and strength, my roots. But seeing us all grown up and there together, I turned my family tree in God's direction. In his light

I realized my roots are more than a mere bloodline binding me to these people in history. The only bloodline that binds us forever is the one flowing from Christ. These people I love so dearly are not my roots at all. They, like me, are mere branches, offshoots from the vine of Christ, symbols of one generation, and then another, and another nourished through the vine rooted in God's love.

Grandpa prayed with his life, and in spoken prayer he always claimed the name of Jesus as the only name by which we can be saved. And when he prayed at family gatherings, he ended each prayer with a blessing on us all, "May we all be found faithful until the coming of Christ."

I remember a sense of anticipation waiting for that last line to come to rest on me. That legacy of a life of prayer has not been uprooted from me or my family with Grandpa's passing. Now I see it has produced dozens of faithful offshoots, new branches as vibrant green as the summer-soft memories of my childhood in the color of my tapestry.

Unceasing prayer abides in Christ.

WEAVINGS
Now fear the LORD and serve him with all faithfulness. . . .
Then choose for yourselves this day whom you will serve. . . . But as
for me and my household, we will serve the LORD. JOSHUA 24:14-15

"By clinging, then, we come to know that heaven is not only
later on, but has somehow already begun, and that the
kingdom is at work in us with a silent greening, shooting up like
spring while there is snow still on the ground."
Emilie Griffin, *Clinging*

❖   ❖   ❖   ❖

Where is Christ in the history of your life? Is he out on the fringes as one of the spokes, or in the center like a hub of the wheel?

Epilogue

I always knew there was more to a prayer life than grace at dinner and bedtime prayers of childhood. But I'm just now learning there is also nothing more holy than meeting God in those routine matters of daily living. The kitchen table where we join hands to pray, or the side of a bed where my parents prayed with me and I pray with my children are sacred symbols of turning my life toward God. It's in such places that I cry out, "Emmanuel! God with us!"

It's been a long time since I've bemoaned my inability to turn to God on any given day. Looking back at my life thus far, I realize two things: First, the tapestry is far from complete. There is still much weaving to be done, and I know God is faithful to complete it. Second, the tapestry which I always perceived as something I could hold up and show who I am is, in fact, not an external ornament at all. The tapestry is woven in the secret places of my heart. It's as Paul said in 2 Corinthians 4:16, "Though outwardly we are wasting away, yet inwardly we are being renewed day by day."

May God bless you with rich colors, textures and beautiful patterns of his love as he weaves a life of prayer through the tapestry of your heart.

Resources

Whenever I pick up a book on prayer, I always feel a special connection to the author. I know that what they write comes out of their own prayer journey.

The following books are a few of my personal favorites that have helped me develop a life of prayer. Some relate directly to the subject of prayer; others are devotional books; and still others Bible studies. Obviously the list is merely a next step and not an inclusive listing of resources. These are the books—some classics, some newly released—that I have learned from and continue to refer to. Have fun discovering other treasures on your own. But above all, test your reading in the light of Scripture, and pray your way through each writing.

Books on Prayer

Bounds, E. M. *The Reality of Prayer.* Grand Rapids, Mich.: Baker Book House, 1991.

Brother Lawrence, *The Practice of the Presence of God.* Springdale, Penn.: Whitaker House, 1982.

Dean, Jennifer Kennedy. *Heart's Cry: Principles of Prayer.* Birmingham, Ala.: New Hope, 1992.

———. *The Praying Life.* Birmingham, Ala.: New Hope, 1993.

Foster, Richard. *Prayer: Finding the Heart's True Home.* New York: HarperCollins, 1992.

Griffin, Emilie. *Clinging.* New York: McCracken Press, 1994.

Johnson, Jan. *Enjoying the Presence of God.* Colorado Springs, Colo.: NavPress, 1996.

Murray, Andrew. *With Christ in the School of Prayer.* Springdale, Penn.: Whitaker House, 1981.

Norris, Kathleen. *The Cloister Walk.* New York: Riverhead Books, 1996.

Rhodes, Tricia McCary. *The Soul at Rest.* Minneapolis: Bethany House, 1996.

Devotional Reading

Blanch, Stuart, and Brenda Blanch. *Learning of God: Readings from Amy Carmichael.* Fort Washington, Penn.: Christian Literature Crusade, 1985.

Chambers, Oswald. *My Utmost for His Highest.* Westwood, N.J.: Barbour, 1935.

Fischer, John. *On a Hill Too Far Away.* Ann Arbor, Mich.: Vine Books, 1994.

Hazard, David, ed. Rekindling the Inner Fire Devotional Series. (Readings by various classic writers). Minneapolis: Bethany House, 1991-1995.

Mains, Karen Burton. *With My Whole Heart.* Portland, Ore.: Multnomah, 1987.

Nouwen, Henri J. M. *The Way of the Heart.* San Francisco: HarperCollins, 1991.

Thomas à Kempis. *The Imitation of Christ.* London: Penguin, 1952.

Tozer, A. W. *The Pursuit of God.* Harrisburg, Penn.: Horizon Books, 1976.

Study Books with Chapters on Prayer

Blackaby, Henry T., and Claude V. King. *Experiencing God.* Nashville: Broadman & Holman, 1994.

Foster, Richard. *Celebration of Discipline.* San Francisco: HarperCollins, 1988.

Heald, Cynthia. *Becoming a Woman of Prayer.* Colorado Springs, Colo.: NavPress, 1996.